Goli

Goliath Birdeaters as Pets.

Goliath Birdeater Tarantula book for care, handling, diet, housing and myths.

By

Adam Burton

Chapter 1: General Introduction

There is a lot of misguidance about Goliath Birdeaters (GBs). They are venomous; they urticate and their bite is very painful; they don't fall in love with their owners; Goliath birdeaters are this and that. These are some of the negative images given to these species of tarantula by some people. The media aggravate the concerns by demonizing them. Why on earth should somebody keep an animal surrounded with such negativity as a pet? This may be the question looming in your mind. But the truth is that Goliath birdeaters are interesting pets to keep.

They are becoming popular pets, as we shall see later in this book. Today, many people have an interest in this species of spider. A lot of tarantula forums and organizations have been established in different parts of the world. Despite the dark sides of having one in your home, there are a number of reasons why having this giant spider as a pet is beneficial. In this chapter, I am going to tell you the drawbacks and advantages of keeping one or more in your home.

Dangers of Keeping a Goliath Birdeater as a Pet

If you are a terrarium enthusiasts planning to keep a goliath birdeater or any other species of tarantula spider in captivity, you should not forget the fact that they are wild invertebrate animals and cannot be tamed like some other animals. Generally, no species of spider can fall in love with the keeper no matter how much time they devote to taking care of the animal. The same is true of the goliath birdeater. I have been a spider enthusiast for many years.

I have always treated my GBs with tender loving care but I have not seen anyone that rewards my kindness with love. They are always fast and aggressive when they feel threatened. So, if you are keeping any species of tarantula, including the largest of them all, you should be ready for their aggression even if your pet appears to be very harmless and gentle.

Consequently, you should not handle this spider otherwise it will throw its urticating hairs on you or even bite you. However, as I will explain later, if you must handle it, ensure that you use the right gear and tools. I normally use long forceps to push them gently in case I have any need to look at them.

You will find in literature that goliath birdeaters and indeed most species of tarantulas are not harmful to humans because their venoms are considered to be too weak to cause any damage to humans. The truth is that they are venomous. They normally kill their prey by injecting their venom into them using their fangs. No matter how weak the venom is, they will normally cause some discomfort to any person they bite. You should always bear in mind that if you are bitten by a tarantula, it will be as if a bee stings you. If you have been stung by a bee before, I don't need to tell you how painful the stinging is.

Apart from the pain, their fangs are strong and big enough to tear your skin. Goliath birdeater's fang are as big as the canine of some cat species. With this, you can imagine how deep their bite can go in the flesh. The best way to forestall any possible attack or bite from your tarantula is to leave them undisturbed or reduce contact with your spider.

Note that even though goliath birdeaters do not have venom that is deadly to human beings, there are certain species of tarantulas that have dangerous venom and they also move very fast. Typical examples of such species are the Cobalt blue (Haplopelma sp.) and Startburst baboons (Pterinochilus sp.). So, if you are interested in keeping any other species of tarantula, it should not be the aggressive species, especially if you are a beginner in giant spider husbandry.

Though tarantula husbandry is growing in popularity nowadays, not much is known about these giant spiders. This is one fact that you have to bear in mind before you go into it. People around you may not understand you and may not encourage you. You will look unconventional and odd to them. Only a few people will listen to your stories when you talk about your experiences in spider husbandry. If you are the type that does not stand their ground even when their beliefs and practices are not accepted or are not popular, you may give up your dream of raising a giant tarantula.

So, bear in mind that you are going into an unconventional area. In case you are not willing to continue for any reason, I advise you to sell your birdeater to another enthusiast. You can also give it away if you like. But do not release the spider to the wild.

Survival rate of goliath birdeaters and other species of tarantula when held in captivity is low for a number of reasons. In the first instance, they are highly sensitive to temperature and weather changes. I will be discussing their housing requirements later, but you should bear in mind that goliath birdeaters from different climatic regions may not survive under the same temperature. Each one has its habitat requirement. So, it is not enough to order one from any spider store. You have to make sure that you are able to maintain a suitable temperature, otherwise it will die.

Another risk of keeping tarantulas of any species in captivity is that their mortality rate during moulting is very high. I am going to discuss moulting in detail in another chapter. But suffice it to mention that it is an important biological process and occurrence in tarantulas through which they grow and regenerate damaged tissue. Despite its importance, it exposes these invertebrates to dangers. It makes them vulnerable to predators and even to their prey. During moulting, they are powerless and can be killed by certain insects and rodents. A good number of them, especially spiderling, lose their lives during this process. The only means to ensure that they survive this natural occurrence is to offer them more protection. Keep their cage secure and free from invaders. Place their cage in a location where children cannot get to. Tell any adult that comes to view your spider moult to lock their cage after viewing them. Besides the fact that they can bite, they can also release their hair in self-defence.

Goliath birdeaters have fragile bodies. Their abdomen is very large but it is fleshy and soft. Their chances of rupturing or tearing when they fall are very high. It is like throwing a bubble on the ground. Note that they are not good climbers like certain species of spiders. So, falls can result in their death or serious injuries to the animal. Sometimes, they may fall down in an attempt to escape captivity.

They may even fall from the hands of their owners who handle them. You can protect them from falls by having a well protected cage with the most suitable environment so that they will not attempt to escape. In this way, you will render any attempt they make to escape captivity a failure. Secondly, you should not handle them at all. If it falls down and the abdomen is ruptured, there is not much you could do to save them from death.

Keeping a goliath birdeater can cause some real problems to your household even when you are careful. The spider defends itself against perceived aggressors by flicking its urticating hairs. The hairs are very tiny and can float in the air. If the animal flicks these hairs, they float in the air and this pollutes your environmental air. The hairs can cause havoc days after they were released by the animal. The real problem comes when they enter the delicate mucous membranes of the mouth or that of the eyes.

You can also breathe them in. When they enter the eye membrane, they can cause inflammation. So, the best way to prevent this from happening is to keep the cage closed. Put on gloves when you are cleaning the cage. After doing any work in the cage, wash your hands. Don't touch your eyes or any other sensitive organs of your body until you have washed your hands. This is because the urticating hairs are tiny and can be trapped by the hands. By washing your hands and rubbing topical cortisone cream on, you will eliminate the hairs and the possibility of them getting into your sensitive organs.

Last but not the least is the problem of differentiating goliath birdeaters from other species of tarantulas. Indeed, beginners in tarantula husbandry who want to keep the bird eating spider may find it difficult to differentiate it from other species of tarantulas. Tarantulas generally have a similar anatomy and structure that you cannot easily make a distinction between them based on their physique and anatomy. Besides, most literature describes them as large, brown and hairy spiders, as most of them share these common characteristics. Thus, you may not be able to differentiate a goliath birdeater from other species of giant spiders based on what you read. Their photos will also be of no help to you because of their similarities.

You need to be well experienced in tarantula husbandry in order to be able to make a distinction between these species of spider. In other words, in order to identify a goliath birdeater or differentiate it from other species of tarantulas, you will rely on the expertise of an experienced arachnologist or experienced tarantula enthusiast. Alternatively, you have to be familiar with them in the first place.

Based on these issues raised above which are experiential, I will not recommend goliath birdeaters for beginners. You can begin with other softer species. However, this does not mean that they are the most aggressive species. Even though they are very active, they don't normally bite. Sometimes, I will leave my cage open as I work in and around it. My spider will crawl and hide in a corner without attacking me. This is quite unlike the Thailand black, which I have also kept. They are very aggressive and will attack anything. The major problem with goliath birdeaters is their high sensitivity to cage conditions. Secondly, they are very large. Their size makes handling difficult.

Why Should I Keep a Goliath Birdeater

Is there any reason why you should keep goliath birdeaters considering the above mentioned concerns? Yes! I have successfully kept goliath birdeaters from spiderling to the adult stage. I believe many other people have also done the same. The number of people going into tarantula husbandry is growing nowadays because of the advantages derived from it. Don't be apprehensive of the above mentioned disadvantages. You will always succeed if you are able to apply the tips contained in this book. Here are some of the reasons why you should consider getting into goliath birdeaters.

Not messy pets

A lot of pets are messy. This is one of the problems encountered by many pet keepers. You have to contend with the problem of cleaning the faeces and urine of the pets. Sometimes, it takes a hell lot of time to clean the mess. But if you are keeping a goliath birdeater, you will not encounter such a problem. It is not messy at all. Their excreta are liquid-like but they dry quickly. Additionally, they don't smell and are not messy. So, you can easily clean it off.

Besides, you don't require many tools to do the cleaning. Just a brittle brush will do the magic for you. Again, cleaning is not done regularly. You may do the cleaning once every 4 to 6 months or whenever you feel that it requires cleaning. However, you have to clean the water dish regularly to forestall the possibility of mould developing inside it. If you don't clean it, insects that drown in it will also make it mouldy. Check the water to see if it has any crickets or insects inside it. Scrub the water dish and refill it with clean water. Replace the substrate if there is any need for that. Make sure that you wash the tank in and out. You are done and that will carry you for a long period of time.

Goliath birdeaters are not the type of pet that will litter your home with unwanted particles. They cannot dirty your sofas or bed with mud. They are not the type of predators that will bring dead rodents on your back porch. No pollution of any kind can be caused by these giant spiders, unless they release their urticating hairs to the air. They need only a cage or container to live in.

Inexpensive type of husbandry

Another reason why you should consider going into tarantula birdeater husbandry is because it is not an expensive venture by all ramifications. First, you may not purchase your goliath birdeater from spider stores. You can hunt for one in the wild by yourself if it lives in your location. But if you must purchase it by yourself, it will not cost you a fortune to get one. Secondly, Goliath Birdeaters do not eat much. It is not expensive to feed them. One or two crickets will be enough for tarantula birdeaters every week. But there are other things that you can give to your pet, which I will tell you later.

Regardless of what you want to serve to your pet, you will not have to break the bank in order to get their food. Outside food, the only thing your spider will require is water. With food and water, your spider will be fine insofar as their habitat is conducive and has the right temperature and humidity. In sum, goliath birdeaters have low maintenance and will not require your attention. In fact, it is advisable to leave your spider undisturbed for the reasons given above.

Makes for a captivating sight

It can be interesting and impressive to watch a Goliath birdeater kill prey during meal time. Many animal enthusiasts spend time watching wildlife on the television via channels like Nat Geo Wild and others. If you have a tarantula birdeater, you will have the opportunity of enjoy a live view of a giant spider hunting for and killing prey. Besides, spider husbandry provides you with the opportunity of learning the fascinating behaviour of small exotic animals. It is a veritable means of bringing nature into your home.

With a goliath birdeater growing in a cage in your home, you will not have any need to go to look for a giant spider in a zoo.

Do You Need a License?

It seems spider husbandry is not regulated or prohibited in most countries. This is because unlike other common pets, many countries' have specific laws regarding goliath spiders as pets. Still, the only way to really be sure is to do your research. In the US for example, licensing laws and permits regarding pets are usually determined by the states or local government and these can change over time and quite quickly at that. So, I will advise you to find out from your local authorities what the regulations are for the keeping of Goliath spiders as pets – as well as their transport and import/export – especially if you plan on travelling with them, or if you are purchasing them from outside your country of residence.

In the US for example, legitimate breeders/exporters usually require a US Fish and Wildlife import/export licence (USFW) before they can ship goliath spiders into the country. Consequently, even if there is no legislation on the keeping of these creatures, it is advisable that you expand your research into local, municipal, city, town and even neighbourhood rules because these might have their unique regulations regarding pet Goliath spiders. Make sure that you are not violating any of your state or local laws.

Myths about Goliath Birdeaters

Goliath birdeaters and other species of tarantulas exhibit certain behaviours that surprise and scare people. They are nocturnal hunters. They appear, kill and disappear into the night. They are giant spiders but their manner of walking is quite different from those of other species of spiders. They walk like robots and in a mechanical manner. Given the mysterious nature of these spiders, it is normal for people to attribute a lot of unproven characters to them.

It is a widely held conception that goliath birdeaters and other tarantulas are deadly and venomous. Because of this belief, they are dreaded and feared by many people. But the truth, as mentioned above is that these spiders contain venom which is less potent as to kill a man even though they paralyse their prey by injecting these venoms into them. The degree of the potency of these venoms differs from species to species.

The origin of this myth could be traced to Taranto, a small town located in southern Italy. In 1370, there was an outbreak of a mysterious epidemic, which the town dwellers believed was caused by the bite of a large spider known to scientists as Lycosa tarantula and commonly referred to as hairy wolf spider. The spider then was referred to as Tarantula, probably derived from the name of the village. The only cure to the disease as it was believed then was a wild type of music and dancing.

However, it was later discovered in 1600s that wolf spider was not the cause of the epidemic. However, the European colonisers and explorers discovered more species of spiders, which were larger and hairier than the wolf spider. They referred to these giant and hairy spiders as tarantulas. This is why many people now classify all hairy and large spiders as tarantulas. But in reality, only the members of the family Theraphosidae, to which the goliath birdeaters belong to are Tarantulas.

However, this myth has not completely fizzled out in the society today. Many superstitious folk people from different parts of the world still kill giant spiders believing that they are poisonous. Some people also make delicacies with them. This hostile attitude towards tarantulas, including goliath birdeaters is one of the reasons why they are going into extinction. But experts through research have discovered that the bites of most of these giant spiders are of little consequence to human beings. Contemporary science groups them together into a family called Theraphosidae family spiders. Many of them, including goliath birdeaters are becoming common in the exotic pet market.

There is another Greek mythology which tells the story Arachne, a woman of stunning weaving skills who challenged Athena the Greek goddess of arts and crafts to a weaving contest. Arachne skills were so great that she was able to create a tapestry that was of the same level with those of Anthena. When Athena saw that she could not beat Arachne in the contest, she was annoyed. In annoyance, she broke the work of Arachne. Arachne could not bear that and she wanted to take her life but the goddess pitied her. To save her life, she turned her into a spider. It was believed that giant spiders are her offspring and got their weaving skills from her.

These are not the only myths about spiders in general and tarantulas in particular. Various cultures have their myths. For example, there are the Pima myths, popular among a number of Indian cultures and the Spider Rock myth of the Navajo people that once lived in the Canyon de Chelly National Park. So, if you come across such stories no matter how awful they are, you don't have to be apprehensive of goliath birdeaters and other giant spiders. These are nothing but myths. They are not founded on any scientific research and evidence.

The media helps to destroy the image of goliath birdeaters and other tarantulas. A good number of unfounded fears and stories about these giant spiders arise from the negative image given to them by the media. Tarantulas have featured in many Hollywood movies and television programs. What the movie industry has done to these innocent arachnids is capture this popular joke among horror movie enthusiasts *"The Tarantula That Ate Tokyo."* In most of these movies, they are presented as scary, deadly and hairy. Consequently, many people think that their bite can kill human beings. The playwright of these movies attributed characters to these creatures that are unrealistic and in many instance direct opposite of their real nature.

The Truth!

Tarantulas, including goliath birdeaters, are not actually what they are said to be. As we shall see later in this book, the real tarantula birdeaters are not the cause of tarantism, as suggested by the ancient Italian myth. They didn't eat Tokyo as the movie made us to understand. They have no capacity to embalm towns and people. They are innocent of the numerous accusations levelled against them, even though they have their own lifestyles. They are only victims of slander, false accusation and misnomer. In reality, nothing is known about their origin. Nobody can say with certainty the forest or swamps where the first tarantula evolved from or where they originated. Nothing is known about their evolution, except a few ghostly clues. All that is known about their origin is that they evolved from a stock of animals, which since over a billion years became differentiated from a more familiar branch of the animal kingdom.

The evolution of their ancestors is unique and different from the evolution of the rest of living things on earth, even though it was, to a considerable extent, interwoven with the rest in a complex manner. They have their unique lifestyle, which many people considered as odd. Their anatomies and physiologies are unconventional. Goliath birdeaters, like many other species of tarantulas, are not aggressive as the media made us to understand. They will only bite or release their hairs when they are threatened. They are the biggest of all tarantulas in terms of mass. Birdeater spiders are as big as giant huntsman and are tarantulas of epic proportions. So, take time to learn about this species of spider and don't join in the media in their unholy crusade against these innocent giants.

Getting Started: How and Where to Source Information

You can see from the above that there seems to be a conspiracy against the giant spiders, not just by the media but by myths circulated by the traditional folk. Besides, it is quite different from conventional pets like dogs, cats, sheep and others that you can easily obtain information about and help from your veterinarian. So, if you are thinking of going into goliath birdeater husbandry, it is important that you know how to source information and where to obtain help. Here are various means of sourcing information.

Tarantula dealers and stores

A tarantula dealer or pet store is one of the places you can obtain reliable information and tips on goliath birdeater care and housing requirements. Many dealers and stores are highly experienced with the keeping of these giant spiders that they sell. This is because they are also keepers. Selling these spiders also entails keeping them because you have to provide a suitable living environment for them and feed them until they are sold. This is why many can provide you with tips on how to care for your goliath birdeater. Most tarantula dealers will be happy to share their experiences with you, especially if you purchase from their store. However, the problem with this source is that you are likely not going to find all the information you require from a store. This is because you are limited to the experience of the dealer or store owner. In research, it is said that a man of one book is very dangerous.

It will be good that you learn from the experience of different people from different localities. In this way, you will be able to obtain useful information and learn what works for you. Besides, offline giant spider stores are not as popular as other types of pet store. So, if none are located in your locality, you may have to travel far in order to obtain similar information.

Using the Internet

The Internet is a veritable means of obtaining information about goliath birdeaters and other species of tarantula. Today, there are a lot of tarantula enthusiast forums and organisations. If you are a beginner in tarantula husbandry, it is advisable that you join one or two forums. When you have any concerns, just post it on the forum and people give you a reply based on their experience.

Apart from online forums, there are many articles on tarantulas, including goliath birdeaters. You can find articles on how to take care of these giant spiders, how to build them a home, humidity and temperature requirements of their living environment, how to take care of baby birdeater tarantulas, their common health concerns and any other useful information about these creatures. Many tarantula enthusiasts and dealers have blogs where they share experiences and provide tips. Spend some time on the Internet reading these articles. You will definitely find any information you are looking for about these pets from these blogs and articles. However, as usual with the Internet, not every site or blog is reliable. It is very easy to get false information from the Internet, as there is no control on the content posted online. Any person is free to post anything they want. So, you should be very careful if you are sourcing for information from the Internet. The only way to avoid getting false information is to ensure that the site you are using is reliable. Ideally, you should look for information in a blog owned by a popular pet store or a popular spider organisation. Blogs owned by experienced goliath birdeater keepers are also good.

These blogs censor the contents posted on their sites. Besides, they only share contents born out of real life experiences and not imagination of the writers. If you are able to find such a blog, you are likely to get reliable information from them. However, you find that tips shared may sometimes be contradictory as they arise from each keeper's personal experience. The problem is which one of them is correct or at least will suit the reader best. Not all of them are correct. Read as many as you can and choose the most popular ones.

Books
A lot of books on tarantulas in general, and goliath birdeaters in particular, are in circulation nowadays. Some of these books dwell on a particular subject matter while some are on general topics. Having a well researched book on goliath birdeater care will be of great help to you. They contain practical tips born out of experience and research. But before you purchase any book, you need to peruse through it. Check the table of contents to see if the topics you are

interested in are covered in the books. Don't just purchase any book on tarantulas, as not all are meant for beginners in spider husbandry. Some books are suitable for scientific study of these animals and may not provide any useful information about their care. A typical example of a good book on bird eating spiders is this book. But there are other ones on the market. Check Amazon, Google books and other online bookstores, you are likely going to find good books that dwell on the care of these animals.

The advantage of books over other sources of information about tarantulas is that it is easy to find the information you are looking for. Just check their table of contents to see if they contain information on the topic you are interested in. Books also have indexes and a glossary. When reading them, if there are terms you don't know, you can refer to the glossary in order to learn the meaning of these terms. Besides, they are more exhaustive than articles. Authors of most books carry out full research on each topic they want to treat. Thus, they are able to provide comprehensive information on the topic they are treating.

Another advantage of books is that you can access them anytime you want. They are not like blogs that can be wound down or that require Internet connection before they can be accessed. On the contrary, books are on your shelves regularly. You don't have to worry about viruses destroying them. No time to waste in order for your computer to boot. You don't have to worry about driving to the pet store or putting a call through to the pet owner. The major disadvantage of books is that they are more expensive than other options. Not everybody will be able to pay for books, especially hard copies. Thus, if you are fortunate to have one like this, take time to go through the content, you are going to learn a lot from it.

Factors to Take into Consideration before Going into Tarantula Husbandry

The first point to bear in mind before you go into goliath birdeater husbandry is quite different from other kinds of pets. Even among tarantulas, it has its unique characteristics and behaviour. Given their uniqueness and differences, they have their unique housing requirements and survive under different environmental conditions. The kinds of health conditions, parasites and bacteria that affect them are quite different from those that affect other pets. Thus, you must get it right with them and treat them as they should be treated. You don't have to assume anything.

Always start from the basics and from there you progress to a higher level. Bear in mind that nothing about the goliath birdeater is conventional. Nothing comprehensive is known about this species of tarantula as it is the case with other pets. Consequently, don't expect to understand everything immediately. Things may get difficult or more confusing to you. But you don't have to be discouraged. Gradually, you will pick it up and become an expert. In other words, you should get ready for difficult challenges, which you have to overcome as time goes on.

As you are reading this book, other books and articles on goliath birdeaters, jot down important points as they are still fresh in your mind. It will be easier for you to refer to what you jotted down than to refer to your book. Important information includes instructions, tips, scientific names, habitat, distribution and continent as well as country of origin.

Chapter 2: Goliath Birdeater: What Type of Animal Is It?

Many people do not know anything about this species of giant spider. A lot of people, based on its name, erroneously think that it is a type of spider that hunts for, and feed on, birds. The superstitious folk see it as a mysterious creature, which can bite and infect its victims with tarantism. But what type of animal is a goliath birdeater? Does it have other names? Which parts of the world is it found in? Is it a spider and if yes what species of spider is it? In this chapter, I am going provide answers to these and other questions as I describe the goliath birdeater.

Goliath Birdeater at a Glance

Scientific name: Theraphosa blondi

Common names: Goliath bird-eater, Giant bird-eater, Goliath (tarantula) and Giant tarantula

Domain: Eukarya

Kingdom: Animalia

Phylum: Arthropoda

Class: Arachnida

Order: Araneae

Family: Theraphosidae

Genus: Theraphosa

Species: Blondi

Sub species number: one

Group: Arachnid

Habitat: Tropical rainforest

Location: Central America

Origin: Trigonotarbida

Diet: Carnivore

Predator: Tarantula Hawk, Mammals and Humans

Prey: Earthworms, bats, humming birds, rodents, small lizards, frogs, bats and small insects

Sizes: 11 inches (28-30cm)

Weight: 170grams

Life Span: Females – twenty – twenty five years and males: three – six years

Gestation Period: six months

Age of sexual maturity: three to six years

Average litter size: hundred to two hundred eggs

Origin and distribution

Giant birdeaters belong to a group of invertebrate animals called anthropods. They are mainly found in South America and the Amazon Rainforest.

Anatomy

Theraphosa blondi, as it is called by scientists, has a similar anatomy with other species of tarantulas I have noted above. This is why it is very difficult to differentiate giant tarantulas from other species of giant spiders. I am going to give the general anatomy of tarantulas. Let's begin our discussion with the external anatomy of the giant birdeater.

External anatomy of tarantula

Just like other tarantulas, the giant bird-eater has an exoskeleton, inside of which other systems and organs are housed. The exoskeleton is hard. Furthermore, the spider gets its shape from this part. It gives structural support to the animal and also protects the spider from losing fluid and drying out, which will result in their death. Besides, it protects the delicate organs of the body from mechanical injury. It shields the entire organs of the spider, making it impossible or difficult for any infectious agents such as bacteria and fungi or foreign bodies from getting to the vital organs of the body. Most muscles of goliath birdeaters attach to the exoskeleton.

There are certain parts of the body of theraphosi blondi that also extend its exoskeleton. Such parts include the setae, bristles and trichobothria. With these organs, the giant tarantula senses things around it.

Additionally, the exoskeleton has an outward extension, called apophysis (apophyses: plural). It differs from the setae and trichobothria, which I just mentioned. The major difference between them is that the apophyses are not joined to the exoskeleton in any way. Instead, they are simply wings, or continuation of the exoskeleton without any intersection. The bristles are not as big as they are. Another part of the exoskeleton is the entapophyses, which is better known as the apodemes. They seem like small holes which gets deep into the tissue of the giant bird-eater. Like the apophyses, the apodemes are not linked to the rest of exoskeleton. They are a smooth extension of the exoskeleton.

The body

The body of bird eating spiders is divided into two parts, namely, the prosoma, which is the forward part and the opisthosoma which is the rearward parts. The opisthosoma links to the prosoma with its pedicel. Goliath bird-eaters, like other tarantulas when compared with human beings, have no head, thorax or abdomen. The prosoma is like the head and the thorax joined together. This is why a lot of archaeologists refer to this part of the body of this species of spider as cephalothorax. This part of the body of tarantulas is externally made up of the four pairs of legs, pedipalps, eyes and the fangs. But its internal organs are the venoms glands and the nervous centre.

The opisthosoma cannot be called the abdomen in the real sense because it contains the respiratory organs and the heart of the spider. You may notice that some enthusiasts or expert spider keepers use the term abdomen to refer to this part of the tarantula body. They do this for convenience, as it is easier to pronounce than to pronounce the term opisthosoma. So, if you find a book where the term abdomen is used instead of the opsthosma (in some sections in this book, the word abdomen is used in place of opisthosoma), know that they are talking of the opisthosoma. On the back of a tarantula is the carapace, which some older books referred to as the dorsal tergum or tergum. The carapace, which is a dorsal plate, has a pit or dent at the centre called the central apodeme even though it seems to be a depression on the exterior.

There are lines and grooves that embellish the carapace and the central apodeme. On the opposite side of the carapace is the sternum, which is like a shield on the underside of the tarantula. The legs' basal segments link the carapace and the sternum together. The movement of the legs is made possible by the pleura (pleurae in plural) which join the carapace and sternum together. The pleurae are flexible in nature.

The opisthosoma of a well-fed goliath birdeater is swollen with a thin, leathery and pliable exoskeleton covering it. There is a dense layer of bristles in which it is wrapped. At the bottom surface of the opisthosoma of a tarantula birdeater is an obvious plate known as the epigynal plate (it is also called the epigynum or epicene). This plate, which is conspicuously seen on the venter, is held by a pair of book lungs located on the both sides of the forward part. Another pair of book lungs, the anus and the two pairs of spinnerets are located further at the back.

Apart from these parts, there are eight pairs of appendages on the body of tarantulas, namely, chelicerae which can be compared with jaws or mandibles of other invertebrates, fangs used for digging and also to kill and eat prey, pedipalps, and the four pairs of working legs (eight in number).

Chelicerae
Chelicerae, which are found directly in front of the mouth and below the eyes, are two single segment appendages. The venom glands that come out through the fangs and the muscles encircling them are enclosed by chelicerae.

Fangs
The fangs are used by the giant spiders to chew their food. Goliath tarantulas, and other giant spiders in its class, inject venom to their prey with the fangs in order to kill them. They also burrow with this part. They are hollow-like which extend the chelicerae. It is highly flexible and thus, it can go outward or move downward. They can come together, going into the chelicerae.

Pedipalps
The pedipalps are located close to the mouth of the spider. These two appendages help the spider to feed as they use them to turn over

and position the prey the way it will suit them. In male giant tarantulas, the pedipalps perform additional functions. They also serve as the sexual organs for transferring the semen to the females. Before a male becomes sexually mature, these appendages are like boxing gloves as they are expanded. Unlike the males', the females' pedipalps are thin.

The legs

Goliath birdeaters have four pairs of legs meaning that they have eight legs. The legs are highly flexible because of how each is segmented into seven parts. Despite their flexibility and ability to move closer to the body, they cannot be stretched outside of the body. If a tarantula has a need to move the legs or any of the legs outside the body, it has to pump fluid into the leg(s). The legs become extended as fluid flows with pressure building up and relaxing. It is like water flowing through a host. As the water is flowing through, pressure is built and the host becomes stiff and stretched. The pressure relaxes as the water is released. In other words, for a goliath birdeater to stretch or move its legs outward there must be changes in the pressure of body fluid. The reverse is the case when they want to move their legs inward. They use the muscle but do not require changes in the body fluid pressure.

How does a goliath birdeater sense the world around?

Goliath birdeaters, like other tarantulas, have sense organs for sensing the world around them. The first organ to mention here is the eyes. They are external organs, which in most animals are used for seeing. Generally, tarantulas don't see very well with their eyes despite the fact each giant spider has 8 eyes. Each of the eyes has a single lens. The eyes are arranged in two rows with each row containing four eyes. To a considerable extent, these invertebrates sense the world around them with their eyes. With the eyes, they can detect polarised light. Once detected, they will move to a safe location.

Tarantula birdeaters also use the organs of touch to sense the world. Their bristles, which most people refer to as hairs, are their important organs of touch. Their body is covered with hairs, which do not perform the same functions depending on their location on the body. At the trichobothria, which is the lower limbs, are hairs that help the giant spider to detect the weakest air currents. This will help them to know the best location to move to. Thus, these hairs are for orientation. There is another group of hairs on the feet of spider. They help the spider to maintain balance or their footing on the surface, including smooth platforms like glass. They are called scapulae. The defence hairs are on the "abdomen" (recall I said about the abdomen above).

These defence hairs are known as the urticating hair. Many people erroneously think that every hair on the body of these giant spiders are for defence. All hairs on the body of the tarantula birdeaters are not removable. When threatened, they will become aggressive and then flick these detachable hairs to the aggressors using their hind legs. As already mentioned above, you should be wary of the urticating hairs as they can cause skin irritation. They can also cause inflammation when they enter the eyes or when they are breathed in. Consequently, you should be very careful when caring and handling these spiders. Put on your glove and if possible protect your face with a face cover. Remember that they are wild animals and cannot be tamed no matter how well you try to provide for them.

Note that goliath birdeaters and other species of tarantulas in the actual sense do not have hairs. Hairs are exclusive to mammals. No invertebrate or any other animal has hairs. However, I use the term hair here for the purposes of clarity and ease of understanding. The right terminology is bristle, which can be used for any hair-like organs of the spider. It includes parts like trichobothria, setae and spine. You may find that many authors use the term hairs. When you read books speaking of tarantula hairs, know that they are talking about the bristles.

Another important point to take note is that giant birdeaters and other species of tarantulas moult (they shed of their exoskeleton) in order to grow.

The Internal Skeleton and Systems of the Giant Tarantula

The internal anatomy of giant spiders comprises of a skeleton on which the muscles are attached. The skeletal system also provides the platform on which other internal systems of tarantulas are built on. Here are the various systems in the internal anatomy of this species of spiders.

The nervous system

The goliath birdeater has a nervous system which consists of ganglia (two collections of nerve cell bodies). These ganglia have nerve fibres, which connect the system to other internal organs of the spider. The nervous system is located in the cephalorthorax or prosoma. The nervous system helps in the transfer of messages between the body and the organs.

Respiratory system

The main respiratory organs of goliath birdeaters are the book lungs, which are four in number. Each lung comprises 15 or more thin sheets of tissues folded and organised in a cavity, like pages of a book. The blood vessels provide these sheets of tissue. Each of the opisthosoma has a tiny slit on its side. The slit is also located close to the front side of the opisthosoma. It is through this narrow opening that air enters the cavity. Oxygen contained in the air goes through the blood vessels in the lungs into the blood stream. The giant spider requires moisture to stay alive. The respiration system also helps the spider to obtain moisture in the same manner as described here.

The circulatory system

The goliath birdeater does not have the same circulatory system as humans and some other animals because it is fashioned to suit their blood type, which is referred to as hemolymph. It is quite different from those of human beings. These species of spiders have hearts found along the top of opisthosoma. This important circulatory organ of giant spiders is like a long slender tube that emanates from the nervous system. This means that the function and activities of the heart is coordinated by the nerve cells from this system. Blood flows from the heart through sinuses, which are open passages to all parts of the body. If the exoskeleton is punctured or wounded, the hemolymph will be lost and if it does not stop or if the wound is not healed, the spider will die as a result of short of hemolymph.

Digestive system

Goliath birdeaters have a mouth, which is located under the chelicerae. It plays an important role in the digestion of food, as it is the starting point of digestion. You will be surprised to hear that the mouth of giant spiders is very tiny and shaped like a straw that only liquid can pass through it. It is a sucking mouth. But what happens to the solid food consumed by the spider? Tarantulas consume solid foods but before these foods are taken in, they have to be turned into liquid form. The pre-digestive juices secreted in the chelicerae come through the opening to break down the foods and turn it into liquid-like substances. The liquefied prey is pushed down to what is known as the sucking stomach, which is surrounded by muscles. The sucking stomach situates in the prosoma even though the stomach runs through the entire body's length. The contraction of the muscles surrounding the sucking muscles brings about the sucking action through which the food mixed with the pre-digestive juice goes into the mouth into the intestines.

The digestion of food into finer particles continues at the intestine. It is turned into absorbable liquid, which goes into the blood and circulatory systems of the blood for distribution to the various organs of the body that require it. The food particles that are not broken down are ejected out of the body system. They will turn into tiny balls, which is the faeces of the animal. Goliath birdeaters are clean animals. Thus, they will go to a suitable corner to defecate. The faeces easily dry up. Unlike the faeces of other animals, the excreta of this animal do not smell and it is not messy, as already mentioned above. You can clean up the cage of your spider as suggested above, that is once in a while.

Silk glands

Generally, tarantulas do not live on webs or use the web to trap prey. They are hunters and catch their prey by hunting for them. However, like other spiders, they also make webs. They make webs for a number of purposes such as handling food. They also stay there during moulting. They have the silk glands and spinnerets for weaving the webs. Normally, a giant tarantula has about three different silk glands, which are located in the opisthosoma. The silk used to weave the web is secreted in these glands. Are you surprised to hear that it is secreted? Yes, they are produced and delivered as liquid. However, when it goes out of the gland through the spinnerets, it solidifies to become the web. There are about 2 to 4 pairs of spinnerets in every birdeater tarantula. The anterior pairs are shorter than the posterior pairs, which are finger-like in appearance. The silk from the silk gland is secreted through all the four pairs.

Tarantulas use the silk for different purposes, just like other species of spiders. First, they use their silk to close the entrance to their burrows to keep them protected from predators and to guide against disturbance of any kind. It also helps to alert the tarantula of the presence of an intruder. Tarantulas also use their silk to orient themselves and find their way back to their burrow in case they wander away. The silk in this regard serves as a dragline. When enlarging their burrows, goliath birdeaters normally cover soil with its silks before bringing them out of the burrow.

Tarantulas prepare a cradle for themselves during moulting with their silk. They lay on the mat they prepare for themselves during moulting. The male spiders prepare the sperm web with the silk. This serves as a temporary depository for sperm as they search for their female mating partners. A male identifies a female giant tarantula through the chemical smells of her silk in the entrance of her burrow. The female tarantulas also use their silk to prepare their egg sac, where their eggs will develop. But unlike other species of arachnids, goliath birdeaters don't make snares and traps with it, even though they are very strong. In some cultures, some fishermen make fishnets for small fishes with tarantula silks. There are also reports of primitive Aboriginal tribes stitching wounds and cuts with silk from tarantulas.

Note that the silk of these invertebrates does not lose their strength and durability very easily. If your tarantula has made a web in its cage, it can remain for up to a year or more. Even if you don't remove them, they are not likely to cause any health hazard to you because bacteria and fungi hardly survive in it. The silk is rich in protein but despite its high protect content, it is consumed only by a few other animals. I will advise you to remove the silk left by your pet tarantula when they have accumulated. Though some species of spiders consume their webs when they have degraded, tarantulas rarely consume them. However, as they are feeding on their prey, they may consume a little bit of their web together with their foods.

The reproductive system
There are both male and female goliath birdeaters and each has its own unique reproductive system. The male has a pair of testis, which has an external opening through which semen flows. The testis situates in the opisthosoma. Similarly, a female giant tarantula has paired ovaries also located in the abdomen. The ovaries are paired and they come with an opening that runs through it. The sperm is transmitted to the female by the male during coitus and it goes into the ovaries through the epigastric furrow.

Reproduction and Perpetuation of Kind
Goliath spiders are giant spiders but like every other living thing, every mature giant tarantula starts life as an egg, which hatchs into a tiny spiderling. As with other living things, they don't live forever. They will also die one day or be eaten by a predator. Here, I am

going to tell you a little bit about reproduction and lifecycle of the Theraphosa blondi. I will start with reproduction.

Reproduction

Reproduction, through which every living thing perpetuates their kind, is somewhat a delicate exercise in goliath birdeaters. You may be wondering what I mean by "it is a delicate exercise." Indeed, it results in the death of a member of the species. I will explain. Normally, it takes a goliath birdeater about 3 to 6 years in order to mature into a full grown adult with functioning reproductive and sex organs. When a female is ready for mating, it will send chemical signals, which will attract the male. The males follow the chemical signal emitted by the silk of the female in their burrow. While searching for a mating partner, if two males approach the burrow where the female is, they will definitely engage themselves in a deadly battle, which may result in the death of one of them. Anyone that wins the battle will gain the mating right. However, the mating can be a suicidal exercise. The female goliath birdeaters are bigger than males and they are more aggressive. As already mentioned above, tarantulas have impaired visions, even though they have eight eyes. They become aware of their environment with their senses.

Thus, as the male is approaching and enticing the female, she may take him to be an intruder or prey and can attack and kill him. But after a brief moment of mating, the male leaves for safety to avoid being killed by the mating partner. The male is gifted by nature with a special type of mating hook, which protects it against the dangerous fangs of the female. The female becomes fertilised after the mating. She will lay about 100 to 200 eggs in a couple of days after copulation.

Some females can also reserve some portion of the sperm injected by the male mating partner for about 15 months. The sperm cells will fertilise her again for the production of another set of eggs. The eggs are contained in an egg sack. Female giant tarantulas normally lay their eggs in their burrows but they guard their eggs jealously in a number of ways. First, they seal their burrows with their sticky silk. They stop hunting in order to guard the eggs aggressively. They also protect the eggs from parasites and predators by attaching some of their urticating bristles on the egg sack. The egg is the first stage in the lifecycle of a giant spider.

Note that male spiders don't have a penis for introducing the sperm into the female during mating. There are also no organs similar to the penis that performs such a function. A male giant tarantula copulates with the appendages on the end of the pedipalps. It introduces the sperm using this appendage.

Regeneration

Giant tarantulas, just like other species of spiders, have the ability to regenerate a lost limb during the successive moults. The length of time between the period the limb was lost and the next moulting determines the initial size of the lost limb. The limb will be longer in size if this period is longer. The reverse will be the case if the period is shorter. But regardless of how small the limb is in size at this initial stage, it is as complete and fully formed as normal size limbs. It will gradually enlarge in size at the successive moultings, within a period of two to four years. Growth here is all about growth in size and not in terms of development of organs.

Apart from the legs, some other appendages to the body of the goliath birdeater can also regenerate themselves when they are damaged. It is possible for the spider to break its fang's tip if it is hit against a hard surface or even during moulting sometimes. But with a broken fang, the tarantula can feed normally. However, the fangs will also regenerate themselves as explained above.

Lifecycle of a Goliath Birdeater

Every tarantula undergoes three stages in life. Below are these stages.

The egg

Every giant birdeater begins its lifecycle as an egg. The egg sack containing the egg is technically called chorion. It can be likened to an eggshell. The egg at this stage looks like a bead or small ball. It varies in colour. It can be yellow, milky or cream-colored. The embryo will start to develop if the egg is actually fertilised. As it is developing, its chorion will be shaded. The chorion, as already mentioned, is produced by the mother and not the developing embryo. Thus, hatching or shading of the enclosure is not taken as moulting in the strict sense. The shaded chorion is not considered as the exoskeleton of the baby and therefore the process is not regarded as ecdysis. The shaded chorion is also not called exuvium.

The developing spiderling, at this stage when the chorion has been shaded, is regarded as post embryo. It cannot crawl around at this level even though it can move its appendages. It looks like a mite gummed to the egg. It does not hunt but obtains its nourishment from the nutrient contained in the egg. Gradually, the post embryo will develop to become a spiderling, which will moult its exoskeleton. This is the first moulting and it brings this stage to an end and begins a new stage in the developmental cycle of a goliath birdeater. In all, the eggs may require about six to seven weeks to hatch.

Spiderling

Spiderling will begin to move about and even leave the burrow after their first moult. Unlike the adult giant tarantulas, they are very tiny at the point of departure from their mothers' burrow. They are highly fragile and can become prey to bats, birds, snakes, insects, frogs and others. This is why a lot of them die in their infancy. Hundreds are hatched but only a few grow into adulthood. Note that they do not leave the burrow immediately after hatching. Their mothers look after them for a couple of weeks before they move out to start their individual lives. As already noted above, spiderlings cannot use their reproductive organs because they are not yet mature. Males can only be differentiated from females after they have matured into fully grown adults.

Adults

At the completion of their first moulting, the young giant tarantulas continue to moult when it is time to do so. They moult more frequently than adults. It will take a spiderling about 2.5 - 3 years to become a fully fledged adult. Male goliath birdeaters do not live longer. They die shortly after maturity. It has a lifespan of about 6 years. The female on the other hand have a longer lifespan. Some may live up to 15 years while some have 25 years lifespan. Adults goliath birdeaters are available in different colours, which range from light to dark brown. Their legs have faint markings.

Behaviour

Giant birdeaters are unique in their behaviour, which makes them distinguishable from other species of spiders and tarantulas. It is important that you understand how they behave before you can begin to keep them in your home. The first point that you must bear in mind is tarantula bird-eaters are not a social type of invertebrate. They prefer to live a solitary life. Not much is known about their mode of communication because of their solitary lifestyle. Males fight each other in order to gain an exclusive mating right. They also defend their burrows against invaders and their own kinds. Males do not live with females for fear of being killed. They only go to the female for mating and after mating they quickly leave for their lives otherwise they risk being killed.

Similarly, the females can kill the males that mated with them, as they are very aggressive. They guard their burrows, stay for several weeks with their spiderlings before they leave burrow. When their burrows are occupied by a predator, they don't create a new one. Instead, they wander about in search of an abandoned burrow. This exposes them to danger, as they can be killed by predators during the search. They are dead if they wander into a burrow of a predator like a big snake or large centipede. Because of their solitary lifestyle, the assumption of biologists is that they have very poor communication rapport between themselves. They either kill a prey or they get killed.

Another remarkable behavioural pattern and lifestyle of this species of tarantula is that they are nocturnal invertebrates. Like other nocturnal animals, they sleep and rest during the day in their burrows but at night, they come out. They hunt rather than using the web as a trap. They are aggressive especially the female, yet they are lazy when it comes to moving about. A giant tarantula cannot walk a far distant away from home. They can only cover some feet away from home before becoming tired. This may be because of their size. The goliath birdeater is known for the hissing sound it makes when it is frightened or stressed. The hissing sound is produced by the spider by rubbing the bristles under its legs in order to release the urticating bristles.

Difference between Male and Female

The giant birdeater is not like most animals that you can easily sex or differentiate between the genders by mere looking at them. Just like other species of tarantulas, you cannot differentiate a male giant tarantula from a female by the shape of their abdomen, their behaviour, how they hunt, how they burrow and store their foods and things like that. All tarantulas have similar appearances and shapes. This is why it is difficult for a beginner to guess the sex of a spiderling or even an adult giant birdeater. However, it is not an impossible task to sex them.

All spiderlings look alike without any distinguishing characteristics or parts. The male goliath birdeater develops a special type of hook as an appendage on the pedipalps when it is fully mature. This normally occurs during its final moulting. This appendage is known as tibial. The presence of this hook is a sign that a male can now mate. It uses the tibial to hold the fangs of the female during mating so that it will not be bitten by the mating partner. Another important distinguishing part of a male tarantula is the bulbs. *Emboli,* as it is also called, are found on the pedipalps. They are like the sexual organs because male use them to transfer their sperm web to the female.

Another and a more accurate method of sexing a tarantula is to check for the extra spinneret before the epigastric furrow. This is called fusillade. The production of the sperm web is done in this organ, which is not available in the female. The fusillade is present in all male spiders, including young tarantulas. However, a naive or inexperience keeper may not be able to find this organ. An expert tarantula keeper can find this part. It does not require the use of a microscope. With the naked eye, you will be able to see this part. The epigastric furrow is the part that is linked to the epiandrous glands where the silk is produced. So, check for it before this organ. You will likely find it.

In contrast to males, female tarantulas have spermathecae where the sperm released by the male during mating is kept. It is the females' sperm storage receptacle. You can look for this sexual organ in the exoskeleton of your tarantula. But you will require a stereo dissecting microscope in order to find this organ though it can be seen with the naked eye if the tarantula is large. The spermathecae situates in the interior of the opisthosoma above the epigynum, which is the genital opening. The epigynum is found between the anterior book lungs. This part is also moulted along the side with the rest of exoskeleton. So, if you want to sex your tarantula, all you have to do is to check for the presence of spermathecae in the exuvium, that is the moulted skin. If you cannot find it there, it is a clear sign that what you have is a male goliath tarantula.

This method requires experience. So, if you are still a novice, you may not be able to use it. Inexperience keepers can confuse this part with the accessory organs. But spermathecae are basically encircled by the uterus externus.

Note that physically, adult females are not only sturdier and better built than males, they are also larger in size. The difference in size can be significant as well. Females also have a broader chelicerae. However, you cannot sex your tarantula based on these physical differences, because they can fail you. They are not a reliable method. If you want to get an accurate result, you should make use of the methods mentioned above.

However, to get an accurate result, it is advisable that you take time to learn more about the various parts of goliath tarantulas. In this way, you will be able to know the distinguishing parts when you come across them. Knowing them will also help you not to mistake them with other parts. The information provided here about the parts of the tarantula is very scanty. There is a lot to learn about the anatomy of the tarantula. This book is limited in scope; thus, it does not cover much on these parts. So, I will advise you to look for a book that provides detailed information on the anatomy of Goliath birdeaters, or tarantulas in general, to learn about these parts for easy and quick identification. You may find it difficult to sex your tarantula initially but with experience, the task will be much easier for you.

Goliath Birdeater and other Species of Tarantula

Goliath birdeater is a species of tarantula. It is one of the biggest in the family of tarantulas, which are known for their size. Giant birdeaters share certain characteristics with members of it class. Due to these similarities, many people erroneously use the word tarantula to describe every large spider with hair. Generally, tarantulas have hairs and they are large. But they are not just one type of spider. There are close to a thousand species of tarantulas, which are distributed world over including North and South America, Europe and Africa. But each type of a tarantula has its uniqueness and distinguishing characteristics. So, not all hairy spiders are goliath birdeaters. They vary in colour. Some are black in colour. Other colour variants include brown, gray and light colours. They are not of the same size. Some are more aggressive than others. There are also some whose venom are deadly. They have different habitats. There are some that live on trees. Some are also terrestrial in nature. Like that goliath birdeater, there are other species that burrow.

Apart from giant birdeaters, there are other species that you can hold captive in cages. Here are some of the species of tarantula that you keep if you cannot find giant tarantulas.

Species common name	Scientific name	Habitat	Recommended Cage humidity	Recommended cage temperature	Lifespan
Pinktoe	Avicularia	Arboreal	70-80%	70-80 degrees (21-27 degrees), Although, being hardy, they can tolerate temperatures as low as 65 degrees F (18 degrees C) C)	Males: 3 years and females: 10 years
Honduran Curly Hair	Brachypelma	Terrestrial	65-70%	70-85 degrees F (21-29 degrees C	Males: 4 years and Females: 8 years
Rusty Red Baboons	Hysterocrates sp.	Burrowers	70%	70-90 degrees F (21-32 degrees C)	Males 3 - 3.5 years, Females
Orange blue bottle	Chromatopelma cyanopubescens	Arid environment	30-50%	70-80 degrees (21-26 degrees C)	
Ornamental tarantulas	Poecilotheria	Arboreal			
Green Bottle Blue	Chromatopelma cyneopubescents	Semi-arboreal	60%	70-78 degrees F (21-26 degrees C)	Males: 4 Years and females:

Species common name	Scientific name	Habitat	Recommended Cage humidity	Recommended cage temperature	Lifespan
					12 years
Pink Zebra Beauty	Eupalaestrus campestratus	Burrower and terrestrial	70%	75-80 degrees F (24-27 degrees C)	Males: 10 years and females: 25 years
Chaco Golden Knee	Grammostolapulchrispes		65%	78 degrees F (26 degrees C)	Males: 5-6 years and females: 15 or more years
Mexican redknee/leg/red rumps	Brachypelma smithi,	Terrestrial	50-60%	70-80 degrees F (21-27 degrees C)	Males: 10 years and females: 30 years

Note that some of these species are not good for beginners because of their aggressiveness nature as well as how venomous they are. There are certain species that you should avoid regardless of your experience level. A typical example of such species is the Chilean Rose Hair, known to scientists as Phrixotrrichus spatulata. The major problem with this species is that it is highly boring. It moves lackadaisically and feels reluctant to attack prey. It is a lazy spider. Many keepers detest it for this attitude, as it does not give them the thrill in watching a spider kill a prey. But they are very gentle and lovely. Besides, they are sold at a very reasonable price and are readily available in pet shops.

Chapter 3: Goliath Bird Eater Housing Requirements

If you want to keep a giant tarantula in your home, one of the things that you must provide for it is a suitable home. Goliath birdeaters and other species of tarantulas are highly sensitive to their environments. If the environment is not suitable, they will not survive. A suitable environment is one that has the best of temperature, humidity, space and substrates. The cage you will provide for them should also meet the lighting requirements and should have a hiding place for the spider, as they don't like being disturbed. In this chapter, I am going to talk about the housing requirements, the cages and their various types and the nitty-gritty of tarantula housing. This is an important chapter because tarantulas in general differ from conventional pets and as such, you will require this background information so that you will not ignorantly subject your pet to a condition that will result in their untimely death. Let's start with the cage.

Goliath Birdeater Cage at a Glance

Setting up a cage for your giant tarantula does not require any expertise. Though there are special and industrially produced cages for burrowers like giant birdeaters, there are various kinds of containers that you can use and some of which may be obtained from home in order to save money on that. The container can be made of plastic or glass. You can also use an aquarium. A sizable plastic shoe box, which can be purchased from a department store or a supermarket, is also another good option for you. Depending on the size of your spider, a plastic shoe box of about 36x18x13cm (14x7x5inches) will be ok.

Regardless of the cage you want to utilise, you should ensure that it meets the space requirements. Considering the size of a tarantula birdeater, a suitable tank should be about 45cm (17.72inches) in length with a depth of 30cm (11.81inches). The cage should not be too wide or spacious. For example, any cage larger than 38 litres (10 gallons) is too wide for a tarantula.

A good cage should be lidded. Goliath birdeaters are skilful escapists. On no account should you keep them in a cage without cover. If you leave your pet's cage uncovered, there are two possible experiences that you are likely going to have. First, when you come back, you will find an empty cage. These spiders don't waste opportunities to escape. So, once, you create such an opportunity, they will seize it. No matter the height of the cage, don't think that a goliath birdeater will not be able to climb to the top. They are strong and regardless of their weight they can climb though not as proficient as arboreal species. Secondly, your pet may end up breaking its limb in attempt to escape from captivity. As already mentioned above, tarantulas have fragile bodies and falls can result in broken limbs. So, don't give room for the spider to attempt climbing the cage in order to escape from captivity.

Giant birdeaters like sitting out in the open. This makes them good animala for display in an aquarium. So, if you want to view them or use them for display, you should use a glass or transparent container but don't leave the container uncovered. If the container that you want use does not have any cover, you don't have to create one. If there is anything to improvise, it should not be the cover. Purchase a cover that gives a perfect fit to your container if it does not come with any. A suitable cover is one made of chicken wire, also known as hardware cloth or hot-dipped, galvanized wire.

A good cage should also be also be well ventilated. Whether you are constructing one by yourself or you're purchasing it from the market, ensure that there is sufficient air circulation in the container. If you are providing it by yourself, all you need is to do is drill some holes by the sides and towards the top of the container that you are using. But you should ensure that the holes are not covered by the lid. They should not be very large as to allow prey, such as a cricket to escape. If you don't have a drill, you can use a medium sized nail to create the holes. Use a pair of pliers to hold the nail and heat it with your gas or stove. Melt the holes on the cage. Each of the holes should be about 3 millimetres (1/8inc) in diameter. Don't make a few large holes. Ideally, many small ones are ok. The cover should also have openings of the same size made by the sides for enhanced ventilations.

It is also of crucial importance that you provide your spider with a hiding place in their cage. You know, giant birdeaters, like other tarantulas, hunt prey by laying ambush. In other words, they wait in hiding until the prey approaches to a distance where they can quickly bounce on it and inject the deadly venom inside it. So, you have to replicate this hunting life of tarantulas in the cage. This makes adaptation and killing of prey easier for the predator.

Types and Sizes of Cages

Giant tarantula cages are commercially available in different types and sizes. Personally, I prefer keeping my tarantula pet in an industrially made container, which is great for display. I will advise you to purchase an industrially made enclosure as they are worth investing in. These cages are built to suit the lifestyle and environmental conditions of tarantulas. Some are made specifically for burrowers while some are made for terrestrial or arboreal tarantulas. Goliath tarantulas are burrowers. So, if you want to purchase a cage, go for one that is made for burrowers. Below are various types and sizes of commercially made cages suitable for giant tarantulas.

Types of Cages for Tarantulas

XL Terrestrial Cage 20x12x12 (LxWxH) inches (50.80x30.48x30.48cm)

This cage, which is sold for about $145 (£107.13), is specifically made for burrowers or ground-dwelling tarantulas like goliath birdeaters. It features a top loading lid, three lockable hasps, eight vents and four hinges. It is big enough to accommodate a very large giant tarantula.

Large Terrestrial cage 16x8x8 inches (40.64x20.32x20.32cm)

This size is also spacious enough to accommodate an adult tarantula birdeater. It is also made for ground dwellers. Its lockable hasps and vents are two and six respectively. It also comes with top loading lid and three hinges. For this size, you should have a budget of about $105.00 (£77.57)

Medium size cage for burrowers

This cage is 13x7x7 inches (LxWxH) (33.02x17.78x17.78cm) in size. This size will be an option for you if you are beginning with a young giant birdeater. It can also be used to house an adult of a considerable size. However, it is not a good choice for large adults. Like the XL and L sizes, it comes with a top loading lid, two lockable hasps, four vents and two hinges. It is sold for $85 (£62.8).

Small size cage

This is a cage of 10x5x7 inches (25.40x12.70x17.78cm). With the dimension of this cage, it is an option for keepers of baby or juvenile giant tarantulas. It has similar features to the other larger sizes mentioned above. It is sold for $65.00 (£48.02).

Apart from sizes, cages are also available in different shapes. There are some that are rectangular or square in shape. Cylindrical containers can also be used insofar as they are big enough to accommodate the spider and that they have the required features such as holes, substrate and lids, as explained above. Since goliath birdeaters are by nature prone to crawling about rather than climbing, the cage does not have to be very tall. Instead, it should have enough floor space for the animal to crawl about. The leg span of the enclosure should be up to 4 inches (10.16cm) or more.

Other types of cages suitable for tarantula housing are as follows:

Globe style spider housing for a spiderling

Acrylic twin vented vivarium

Clear plastic vivarium

Budget twin end vented cage

Twin rear vented housing

Stackable mini vivarium white and many more

Check this site for these cages in case you will like to purchase one, http://www.tarantulacages.com or http://bugzarre.co.uk

Setting up a Cage of Your Own

If you are on budget or you don't have enough money to purchase a commercially made cage, but you are enthusiastic about tarantulas, there is no cause for alarm. You can also establish a cage for them with the following tips.

Get a suitable container, the length of which should be about 4 inches (10.16cm) longer than the leg span of your pet tarantula and 2 times wider than the leg span wide of the animal. There is no rule about the height but it should be commensurable with the length and width of the container. But as a rule of the thumb, don't use a container that is very tall for this species of tarantula. They are natural climbers even though they can climb. But given their weight, any fall from a height spells doom for them. If you are keeping an arboreal species, there is nothing wrong if the tank is very tall. As already mentioned, the size should be according to the weight of the tarantula you want to keep.

Clean the enclosure. Don't keep your tarantula in a dirty container. So, use a mild dish detergent to wash the container to remove dirt. However, it is not necessary for you to go the extra mile in sterilising the enclosure. A simple wash is all you need.

Get your substrate ready. The substrate can be likened to bedding. Different kinds of items or materials can be used as the substrate. You can purchase vermiculite. To save money, you may consider mixing the vermiculite with peat or soil. A mixture of soil and peat can also be used. The depth of the substrate should be up to 2 to 4 inches (5.08 to 10.16cm). Don't use wood chips, especially those of cedar, as your substrate. The substrate provides a burrowing platform. It also soaks up water and spills or moisture.

Shredded coconut husks sold in pet shops are now popular choices for many tarantula keepers because it works very well. It is sold under different names in the form of brisk. Instructions on how to use it are normally given on the pack. So, when you purchase a pack, check the guide on it and follow it. But if it does not come with any instruction, generally, it is very simple to use. Get a bucket of three litres (5.28 gallons) in capacity. Put the husk inside it and fill it up with lukewarm water. Leave the substrate inside the bucket for about an hour so that it will soak up some water. Squeeze out excess water. When it is dampened with water, it can expand up to 6 to 8 times its volume when it is dry. Place the brisk of dampened coconut husk inside the cage. The depth should be up to 2 to 4 inches (5.08 to 10.16 cm) as suggested above. The substrate will dry within some days.

Whether you are using peat, vermiculite, mixture of both or the coconut husk, it is important that you ram it to form a firm pad. I suggest that at this initial stage, you make the substrate moist so you can obtain a firm pad. Don't bother about the moisture as it will dry within a couple of days.

Note that some materials are not good substrate for giant birdeaters even though they may be good for other species of tarantulas. For example, bark chippings are a good substrate for arboreal tarantulas but they are not good for burrowers like the goliath birdeater. This is because they are not good for burrowing. Horticultural vermiculite, which is an inorganic product, may be a good choice for a young burrowing spider but may not be suitable for an adult burrower, as it may find it too light to burrow in it. If you are using such a material, it is important that you tamp it so that it will be well padded. Don't use top soil or potting treated with chemicals such as insecticides or pesticides to avoid killing your spider unintentionally.

You will need a water dish, as your pet will also drink water. First wash the dish. You don't need to sterilise it. Simple washing with soap is enough. Keep it at a corner inside the cage. You can fit the dish inside the substrate, leaving the opening so that it will be easy for the spider to get inside and come out. However, if you cannot recess it into the substrate, there is no cause for alarm. To forestall the possibility of the tarantula drowning in the dish, I suggest that you put a chip of slate or pebble inside the water dish. Pour clean water inside it. Normal tap or drinking water will be ok.

So, don't waste your money to purchase expensive or any special type of water. Make sure that the pebble is not covered by the water. It is necessary that it bulges out. It will serve as a stepping stone for your tarantula in case it falls inside the water dish. The water dish should also be shallow so that if the giant tarantula falls inside it, coming out will not be a herculean task. You should also consider the size and age of the tarantula when providing the dish.

The water dish serves two purposes. First, it is to ensure the environment remains humid, as it should be. Secondly, the tarantula drinks from it.

The next important thing to include in the cage is the hiding place. As I have mentioned above, it is a necessary part of the cage, which will help to turn the cage into the wild. Apart from serving as a hideaway for the stealthy killer, it also uses it as a place of rest and refuge. I have noticed that the giant birdeaters sometimes stay in a hidden place even when there is no prey to hunt. It does not like to be disturbed.

You can use a half hollow log sold in pets' store as the hideout. Other materials that will serve the purpose include a clay flower pot placed at a corner inside the cage and a piece of cork bark. Most new designs of cages come with hiding places. So, if you are planning on purchasing one, I will advise you to buy one with such a feature.

Decorating the enclosure with plastic aquarium plants or silk plants and leaves to attractively landscape the enclosure is a personal choice rather than a requirement and it is not a necessity. A slightly larger cage may be required depending on the amount of vegetation/plants installed. The trade-off is, the more you put in, the more you have to clean.

Now that you have gotten a suitable home for your tarantula, you need to place it in the right location. Not all locations will be conducive for your tarantula. A nice location should be free from noise or disturbance and away from light source, especially bright light. A place that is hot is not good. A warm location is ok. Your tarantula cage should not be kept close to the door or window. Entryways or passages are not the best location to keep the cage. You should also avoid any place where it can be knocked off or knocked down accidentally by a passerby. It is also not good to keep a cage at an edge of a stand or a height or on anything where it can easily tip over or fall at the slightest touch or kick by dog, cat or any other household pet. Keep the cage away from direct sunlight.

Don't keep your spider's cage in an area that is normally sprayed with deodorants, air fresheners and furniture polish as well as insect killing sprays. Although goliath spiders prefer shade and are nocturnal, do not place them in a darkened cupboard or permanently cover them as they benefit from a natural source of daylight and night-time darkness. Goliath spiders are nocturnal. In a nutshell, ensure that your cage is well positioned where your pet will feel secure and unthreatened.

With this, your cage is ok. You can place the tarantula inside it. I will tell you how to go about it later in the next chapter.

The Lighting and Temperature Requirement

As already mentioned, you should not keep the cage of tarantulas under sunlight or close to a bright source. This is because the animal does not like staying in a bright area. Consequently, you should not keep a cage of this species of spider in a light room. Keep it in a dark spot like a garage if you cannot provide a separate space for it. If you want to provide warmth to the spider during the cold period, never use an incandescent light. Such type of heat source can dry out the goliath. A good option is a heating pad or strip, which you can purchase from a reptile pet store. If you need to heat the cage, place the pad at a corner of the cage.

Goliath birdeaters are tropical invertebrates. Like most species of tarantulas, they prefer a warm environment. For them to survive, you need to ensure that the temperature within the cage is within the normal range suitable for their survival. Take temperature readings of the cage. If the temperature is below or above the range of 25 to 28 degree Celsius (77 to 82.40 degree F), you need to bring it within the range by heating it. However, goliath birdeaters are sensitive to temperatures. Sometimes, determining the most suitable temperature for them can be somewhat difficult. This is because each species of tarantula survives mainly in an environment similar to its natural habit. This means a goliath birdeater shipped to another country will still require the temperature of its native country in order to survive. In other words, if you get your giant birdeater, you have to discover the temperature that will work best for the spider.

The range given here should serve as a guide. All you need to do is to heat the cage unevenly. Place your heating pad or mat at a corner or place half of the cage on the mat so that only a portion will be heated. Your tarantula will move towards to the corner that has the most suitable warmth or environment for its survival. Take the mercury reading of that spot. That should be the required temperature for its survival.

You will require a thermometer when heating the cage with a heat pad or mat. This is because the majority of such heating apparatus' do not come with any thermostat for regulating the heat. A thermometer will come handy as you need it to monitor the temperature of the cage, otherwise you may overheat it.

Humidity Requirements

Giant tarantulas live in a humid, moist rainforest. They can only survive under such an environment. Thus if you are keeping a goliath birdeater, you should provide them with an environment that is moist and humid. It is important that you maintain an adequate humidity. You have to be misting the substrate often. To keep the humidity to the required level, you will need a hygrometer. The relative humidity of the cage should be between 80 to 90%. You should be misting the substrate to keep up to the relative humidity.

This is particularly of crucial importance when the tarantula is moulting. Your spider can die if the environment is dry, especially when she is trying to shade the exoskeleton. You can see why it is necessary that you maintain proper humidity. However, when misting the substrate, don't pour water on the tarantula. Avoid soaking the substrate, as too high a humidity level can also have a negative effect on the spider.

Use the hygrometer to measure and keep records of the humidity to ensure that the spider is not subjected to difficult environmental conditions. You should not allow the cage to be mouldy, stale and stagnant. Hygrometers are normally sold in pet shops. They are available at different price tags, qualities and specifications. Some are simple and inexpensive (like the analogue system). The electronic digital types are more sophisticated and expensive. The digital types have more features. There are some that come with digital thermometer. Find one that will suit your requirements and budget. Furthermore, while you try to maintain a humid environment, you should also make the environment healthy. The best way to achieve that is to ensure that there is proper air circulation in the cage, as instructed above.

Cleaning the Cage

Goliath birdeaters are not smelly or messy creatures as they excrete a virtually non-smelling, quick drying fluid. In general, cleaning the enclosure 3 times a year is sufficient. Do not attempt to clean the cage when the spider is present inside. Always transfer your pet into another separate container before you begin to do the cleaning. Remove everything from the enclosure and thoroughly wash it. Replace all the substrate with new and thoroughly clean ones and rinse all the permanent features and items, especially the water dish. The water dish should be cleaned on a regular basis, every other day, or on a daily basis if dead foods (insects) are present. This will prevent the water becoming foul and mouldy.

Can Two Goliath Birdeaters Be Kept Together?

This is one of the most frequently asked questions in many forums by beginners. Personally, I have not tried keeping two goliath birdeaters together. I don't think it is a nice idea to try it whether they are of the same sex or not. Remember that tarantulas in general live a solitary lifestyle, even in the wild. If you keep two together, it is likely that they will fight until one kills the other. However, you may give it a try or experiment on that. Some tarantula hobbyists have argued that certain species of tarantulas can live a communal life and backed up their argument with their personal experience where they succeeded in raising two or more tarantulas of certain species together in a cage. The question is, will the same result be obtained if such experiment is carried out with the giant birdeater? I have not heard or read about any research where two goliath birdeaters were successfully raised in the same cage. This does not in any way suggest that this cannot be achieved. But considering their aggressive nature and solitary lifestyle, I have reasons to doubt its possibility. May be one day I will do the experiment but for now, I cannot advise you to put two tarantulas in a cage. Provide two different cage if you have two different tarantulas.

Chapter 4: Bringing Your Pet Home

In the previous chapter, I dwelled on the housing requirements of tarantulas. But it is not sufficient to just get a suitable house for your pet. You should also ensure that the tarantula species you have is a goliath birdeater and that it is healthy. In this chapter, I am going to discuss how to find one and place it inside a cage properly. Basically, you can either purchase a goliath birdeater from a pet shop or look for one in the wild if they exist in your locality.

Finding them in the Wild

As I mentioned above, goliath birdeaters are not found in all regions. So, trying to catch one in the wild will be an option for you only if it is a species found within your locality. They are mainly found in South America and the Amazon Rainforest. Therefore, it will be an exercise in futility to enter the wild in search of this species of tarantula if you are not living within any of the zones where it is found. If you plan to search for one in the wild, there are two factors to take into consideration, being able to identify one when you see it and problems associated with this option. Let us go through each of these factors one after the other.

Identifying It

You need to be an expert goliath birdeater keeper before you can search for it in the wild. This is because all tarantula species look alike. You may mistake another giant tarantula with goliath birdeater. So, if you are going to use this option, first take time to study the unique characteristics of the giant birdeater that differentiate it from other tarantula species. Here are some factors to take into consideration that will help you to find and identify a giant birdeater when you see one.

Habitat: The first important factor to take into consideration when searching for a giant tarantula is that it lives in burrows. They have the fangs to burrow. But they can also live in abandoned burrows. So, search for their burrows rather than searching for them in other places like on trees. But don't try digging every hole you see in the wild in search of the big spider. There is a sign to show that a tarantula is living in a burrow. As mentioned above, burrowing tarantulas normally cover the entrance of their burrows with their silk, which helps them to know when a prey or predator is coming in.

The male tarantulas also use the chemical signal of the silk in the burrow to find a female ready for mating. So, when you see a hole, look carefully to see if it is covered with spider silk. You can begin to dig the hole if you find the silk, as it is an indication that a spider may be living there.

Time and method of operation: Goliath birdeaters are nocturnal in nature and are stealthy killers. This means that if you want to catch them outside their burrows, you may have to hunt at night for them. They don't go about hunting. They lay ambush or crouch in hidden corners waiting for their prey to approach. They pounce on them as soon as they appear within close range. So, when hunting for one at night, check places that are likely to provide cover for them.

Take note of their physical characteristics: I have taken time to describe a goliath birdeater in chapter 2 above. Go through the chapter all over again to master the physical features of tarantula birdeaters. They are large, hairy and of different colours. Take note of their form. As mentioned above, their bodies have two segments, the frontal segment connected to the oval-shaped abdomen through a narrow waist. Like every other tarantula species, goliath tarantulas also are eight legged invertebrates. They have eight eyes on their forehead. The eyes lined in pairs and clustered onto a single mound. The fangs, which normally point backwards and located on the mouth area are also distinguishing features of tarantula birdeater. So, check for the presence of the fang if you see a large spider to see if they look like those of the tarantulas.

Issues with a giant eater caught in the wild

Hunting and catching a tarantula in the wild by yourself is a veritable means of cutting cost. However, there are some problems associated with this, which I need to mention here and warn you of before you can decide whether to use this option or not. The first problem with wild-caught goliath birdeaters is that it is almost impossible to determine their age. You may catch one that is close to the end of its lifespan or one that looks older than its age. There is also the problem of infection and illnesses contracted while in the wild. If you are unlucky, you may end up catching a giant tarantula suffering from dehydration, poor health and inactivity which may be caused by a parasite infection and other illnesses contacted while in the wild.

Another issue with these wild-caught adult goliath birdeaters is that in most cases, their captors keep them in poor conditions during the period they are moved from the wild to their cage or the pet shop where they will be sold. Besides, they are not used to life in the cage and may find it difficult to cope. Due to their high sensitivity to temperature and humidity, a good number of tarantulas caught in the wild die earlier than they should have if they were to be in the wild. Given these problems, I will advise you to go for captive bred ones.

Buying one

If goliath birdeaters are not native to your locality or if finding it in the wild is not an option for you, then you have to order from a pet shop or online. But before you order for one, you should make certain important decisions. First, you have to decide whether you want to keep a male or a female goliath birdeater. Many spider enthusiasts prefer keeping the female gender, as she has a longer lifespan. With a female, you also stand the chance of witnessing how tarantulas make their babies. However, if you don't want to keep a tarantula for years, I will advise you to keep a male goliath birdeater because it has a shorter lifespan.

Choosing the Right Age

Another important decision that you have to make is the age to start with. Both adult and young tarantulas are sold in pet stores. But in general, it is easier to keep an adult than to keep a baby tarantula. So, as a beginner, it may be in your interest to begin with an adult. Here are some of the reasons why it is a good idea to begin with adults:

- Adult tarantulas are more likely to survive life in captivity as their chances of adapting to the cage situation are higher than spiderlings, which are quicker in this regard.

- It is easier to take care of adults than to take care of spiderling. You don't have to provide them with regular nourishment, as you will do to spiderlings.

- It is more captivating watching adults bounce and kill their prey.

- Adults are strong and can defend themselves against certain big animals like lizards, mice and others. Spiderling may not be able to kill some of the bigger prey until they become adults.

- The pains of moulting without doubt affect spiderling more than adults.

If you want to start with an adult tarantula birdeater, you should make sure that your cage is big enough to accommodate it. Kindly refer to the section on cages. However, you can also keep a baby giant tarantula if you are ready to make the ultimate sacrifice. Here, I will share tips on how to keep and care for a baby giant tarantula.

Starting with a Baby Tarantula: Tips

The idea of keeping a baby tarantula is frightening to some people because of the task involved. However, regardless of how tasking it may appear to be, it could be regarded as the most rewarding aspect of it. By keeping a spider, you have learnt and experienced all there is to learn and experience about spider husbandry. You can talk as an authority or as person with wide experience. If you begin with a spiderling, you are better off than another keeper that begins with an adult or an enthusiast that keeps only adults. It is an advantage to you seeing a juvenile spider grow from a tiny creature to a fully fledged adult that can fill the hands. But the experience can become sour if you get it wrong and your spiderling dies without getting to the adult stage. Keep to the basics and you will not have such ugly experience. Here are the tips to help you get started.

Theraphosa blondi at the infant stage has a legspan of about 1 inch (25mm). But with proper nourishment, it will grow and become as large as 10inches (250mm). Keeping a spiderling of such a size is not as hard as many people may believe it to be. The tricks to raising a being of such a size to adult stage is as simple as providing them with ventilation, frequent feeding, a conducive environment and maintaining high cage hygiene to reduce the possibility of infection. Let's look at these requirements one after the other.

Caging requirements for a spiderling
The caging or housing requirements for a baby tarantula giant is similar but somewhat different from what has been said above. The important point to bear in mind is that the cage of a baby tarantula birdeater should not be as big as that of an adult tarantula. It is not the best practice to keep a baby tarantula in a big cage to avoid the possibility of the spiderling not finding the prey. With a small cage, you will also be able to monitor the baby tarantula's feeding and general well being as well as moulting, which is a delicate natural process, especially at this early stage in the developmental process of the goliath birdeater. A 40 gram vial will be enough to accommodate

a baby tarantula. A container of such size will allow enough space for the legs of the baby spider. A container for a spiderling should also contain enough substrate with enough depth for burrowing. If you don't want to use a vial, you may consider using baby food jars or a plastic condiment cup of about 1-2 oz. (30-60ml).

You should ensure that there is enough ventilation in the container so that the spiderling will receive fresh air while in the cage. Create holes by the side or on top of the vial. But if you cannot create these small holes, you should consider using a deli cup of 16 oz (480ml) with insect lids for enhanced ventilation. They are better than vials when it comes to air circulation. Besides, you can add more substrate to it than what you can add in vial. With a larger depth and more volume of substrate in the temporary container, you will not have to be moistening the substrate often, as it will take longer time for it to dry. The insect-styled lid on this type of container helps in keeping flies from entering the home of your tarantula.

A good container for a baby goliath tarantula should be transparent so that it will be easy for you to monitor the cage without opening the cage. Though giant tarantulas live in burrows, they do come out to the surface. So if you use a transparent container, you can see the spiderling when they come out on the surface. Also take note of what's been said above on ventilation. Drill holes by the sides and on the cover. Before putting the substrate in the container, first wash it with water and ordinary detergent. Leave it to dry before you can use it. Get your substrate and fill half of the container with it. Prepare your substrate as instructed above. In addition to any of the materials mentioned above, you can use sphagnum peat moss, garden soil or top soil. You will purchase sphagnum peat moss and horticultural vermiculite from the hardware store and a home centre nursery. I prefer using vermiculite because of its appreciable features. It can retain moisture. Thus, substrate prepared with it does not dry out easily.

Besides, it can easily be tampered and form into a pad. It gives structural integrity to spider burrows. You can mix it with a sphagnum peat in equal amounts. Add a little water so that it forms into a pad easily. If you over add water such that the substrate becomes soaked, you can add more material to take up the excess water. Don't make the substrate too wet, otherwise the spiderling may die in the burrow, as its body is delicate at this stage. No spiderling of any tarantula species, including baby Asian species of tarantula that dwell in humid forests, will survive in a condition of excessive damp. I am always careful when preparing the substrate of the cage for a baby goliath birdeater so that it will not become wet more than it should be. Note that with time, your substrate will begin to dry out. At this point, you have to spray water on it or replace it entirely with a new one. When rehydrating the substrate, don't allow water to touch the spiderling. If you are moving the spider to a new cage, you have to first prepare a temporary safe place for the spider.

Baby tarantula birdeaters are somewhat dependent, like human babies are. So, you should make life easier for them. A baby giant tarantula may not be able to burrow as such will be a difficult task. You can make the task easier for the spiderling. Personally, I normally use a pointed stick or a pencil to create a hole that is about 25mm (1 inch) deep by a somewhat hidden corner of the cage. It will accommodate the spiderling perfectly well. So, when it enters there it will gradually expand it into a perfect burrow. When placing the baby tarantula inside the cage, put the spiderling at a location where it will find the burrow easily. Some baby goliath birdeaters are able to expand the burrow and dig it deeper to the bottom of the container. If your spiderling is so strong as to dig deep, you should count yourself lucky, as it is interesting viewing a spiderling relaxing in its home.

You may not provide a water dish in this container. This is because of the size of the tarantula at this stage. If the environment is sufficiently moist, they will be fine. Ensure that the humidity is within range. Place the container properly and in a location where they are free from a direct heat source. As a rule of the thumb, don't provide the spiderling with external heat sources, only when necessary to up with the temperature. First try ambient temperatures and if the temperature does not improve, you can now introduce an external heat source. If you subject the spiderling to excess heat, it can result in its death. Apart from that, it can facilitate the drying up of the heat source.

Monitor the growth of your spiderling. As days go by, they will gradually increase in size and begin to outgrow this container. Indeed, this initial cage is supposed to be a temporary home. So, you have to move it to a bigger cage when it grows in size. At this stage, it should be treated as an adult spiderling. So, you have to apply the caging tips mentioned in this book as well as the care tips that will be explained in the subsequent chapters. As explained above, a permanent home can be a plastic critter keeper or an aquarium.

Watering and feeding requirements of a spiderling
If you are keeping a spiderling, note that its watering and feeding requirements are slightly different from those of adults. Before your baby goliath tarantula becomes an adult, here's how to feed and provide it with water until it becomes an adult tarantula.

Let me repeat that a spiderling does not require any water dishes to improve the moisture of the cage for hydration of your pet. The baby will obtain water from its prey and the environment. But to keep up with the humidity requirements, you need to ensure that substrate does not lose it moisture and dry up completely. However, as the spiderling is growing, its body water requirements will begin to increase, creating the need for you to provide a dish of water. When do you provide the water dish?

Personally, I do that when the legspan of the spiderling is greater than or the same as a 2-liter soda bottle cap. However, at this stage, I only make use of a cap as a water dish. There are certain items that are not good water sources. Typical examples of such items are cricket gel, paper towels and damp sponges. This is because sponges easily become foul and turn into a breeding ground for bacteria.

As I advised above, you should water with caution if you want to make the substrate damp. In fact, some expert tarantula keepers are not in support of spraying water on substrate because of the danger it poses to the spiderling when sprayed with water. As a rule of thumb, you should be conservative about that. Let me repeat the warning again, you should not spray water on your tarantula directly. Also, don't overdo it so that the substrate becomes soaked instead of damp. After spraying, the container should dry out within one day or two. High moisture content will be creating a veritable condition for the growth of fungi like mould.

Another important aspect of spiderling husbandry is the feeding. In fact, even experienced keepers are careful in this regard. This is because as mentioned above, they are still harmless and are inexperience in killing prey. Some prey can also put up a fierce fight to protect themselves from being killed. However, some baby tarantulas are also aggressive and can kill prey as big as their legspan. Because of the fact mentioned above, some experts suggest feeding them with "pinhead" crickets. Some keepers provide them with freshly killed large crickets. There are a group of enthusiasts that advised keepers to smash the head of a live cricket before providing it to their spiderling. Others suggest cutting a cricket into pieces and provide each piece to a spiderling during meal time. You don't have to kill the cricket or smash its head before providing them. Though baby tarantulas are not skilful killers like adults, they can also kill small insects.

The problem is determining the insect that they can kill. As a guide, provide a spiderling with a cricket or any other edible live insect that is equal or smaller to the size of its body, excluding the legs. Ideally, a cricket that is about a week old will make a perfect meal for a goliath birdeater spiderling. Some keepers feed young tarantulas with fruit flies. But the problem with such prey is that they fly around and the young and inexperienced hunter may find it difficult to make a catch. Another problem with fruit flies is that they are not large. So, one is not big enough to constitute a nice meal for a baby tarantula. Termites and maggots can also be used. I don't use them but some experts do.

After feeding a baby tarantula birdeater, check the cage the following day to see if there is anything left over. Remove all uneaten prey. If you leave a dead cricket for a long time in the cage of your baby goliath tarantula, it will begin to decay. This will create a favourable condition for bacteria and pests to develop in the cage. Besides, it will also make the cage malodorous. If you are providing your pet with live insects, it is advisable that you monitor the feeding habit and behaviour of the insect. This is because tarantulas will not be feeding as they should when their moulting period is approaching. It is risky providing baby tarantulas with live crickets when they are moulting or about to moult. They are week during this period and thus are vulnerable to insects such as crickets. They will become prey to some of their predators. This is why it is important that you monitor your baby tarantula very well to find out whether it is about to moult. Stop providing live insects to the spiderling when it is about to moult or when it is moulting already.

You don't have to feed them regularly or every day. But you should not starve your tarantula. This is because if you don't feed them properly, they will not get the essential nutrients that they required for optimal performance. There are some enthusiasts that will want their spiderlings to grow as quickly as possible. To achieve this aim, these growers provide their baby goliath birdeaters with excess food so that they will be power-fed. However, experts are not in agreement as to whether this practice is healthy or not. It is an acceptable practice in reptile growing. But there hasn't been scientific research on the effect of power feeding on spiderling.

Personally, I don't do that. I feed my spiderling twice or once a week with just one prey per meal.

Note that you should leave your spiderling for a few days before providing it with nourishment when you place it inside a cage for the first time. This will give the animal some time to adapt to the new environment. However, some people feed their spiderling as soon as they move it to its new home.

Handling of a spiderling

I thought of putting this subheading under the next chapter but since I have gone deep with spiderling care, it will be better to complete the discussion on spiderling here. I use the term handling because I lack words to convey the idea. In the real sense, spiderling should not be handled because of how delicate they are. They can easily die. However, from experience, it is possible for a spiderling to escape from the cage. You have to look for them and catch them. Transferring them to another cage may require you to handle them.

When you are cleaning the cage or misting it, you may have to bring the spiderling out of the cage. The issue that I am going to address here is how you will handle the spiderlings, should any of the above mentioned situations arise. On no account should you pick up your baby giant birdeater with the hand. As already mention, at this stage of development, the spiderling is very fragile. Improper handling can result in breaking of a limb. All you need to move the tiny but chubby spiderling to any direction you like is a small paintbrush used by artists. You may also need a trowel, a pair of long forceps or similar tool.

If you want to bring the spiderling outside the cage, simply bend it down so that the opening side will be perpendicular to the ground. Use the brush to lightly direct and lead the small tarantula birdeater out of the cage. Do the same, if you want to bring the spiderling inside the cage. You may also use the trowel. Just lightly brush it inside the trowel and then lightly also drop the tarantula inside its cage. The brush to be used should have soft bristles. Hard bristles may wound the fragile body of the spiderling.

Can I Train My Goliath Birdeater to Love Me?

Many people keep pets like dogs, cats, parrots, reptiles like pythons and others to train them so that they will be perfect companions. Such conventional pets are fond of their owners. With training, they recognise the voice and perceive the body odour of their owners. Given this, it is not quite uncommon for novice spider enthusiasts to ask whether their giant birdeaters can be trained to love them. The answer is basically negative. As already mentioned above, giant birdeaters are, to a considerable extent, aggressive.

They are not social and cannot be trained like conventional pets to love their owners. If you own one, it will be an exercise in futility to attempt to train one to love you, as you will not succeed. Another reason a goliath tarantula cannot be trained is that as an invertebrate animal, its brain is not like the brain of man or other higher animal. It only acts according to the dictates of instinct. If it is not threatened, it will remain calm. But if it is threatened, it will bite. So, if you attempt to train the animal, you are only threatening it and it will simply bite you or fling urticating bristles on you. There is nothing you can do to improve their sociability, as they are not puppy or kitten.

Moulting in Spiderling

Spiderling moults, that is shades its exoskeleton for a number of times throughout this stage of its lifecycle. It is an essential growth process. Without moulting a baby tarantula cannot grow into a fully fledged adult. Normally, the frequency at which this process occurs is very high during infancy. I have kept a baby goliath birdeater that moulted once every month and another that was moulting once in two months during their infancy stage. Regardless of the importance of this growth process, it is a delicate process as it exposes the spider to danger. Tarantulas are normally weak and defenceless when they are moulting. Thus, they can become prey to their food. The way a spiderling is to be handled during moulting should be different from the way an adult should be handled during the process. Here are what you should do or how you should handle the spiderling during moulting.

First point to take into consideration is what I have mentioned above. They are weak during moulting and can be killed by their prey. Another point to bear in mind is that tarantulas don't eat when they are preparing for moulting. Fasting may start some days or up to a week before the beginning of moulting. So, if you observe that your spiderling has stopped eating, don't be in a hurry to conclude that it is suffering from an illness. It may be because it's preparing for this growth process. Take a closer look at the exoskeleton of the spiderling, if the fasting is as a result of preparation for moulting, the spiderling will experience change. Its abdomen will darken. In general, it will become duller in colour. As I have mentioned earlier, no food should be offered to the spiderling during this period. At the completion of moulting, I advise that you wait about two to three days before providing the baby tarantula with nourishment. This will allow it a complete recovering time.

Taking records of dates

If you are keeping several or many tarantulas, I will advise you to have a note book where you will be keeping records of the dates you feed each of your goliath birdeaters. With your record, you will not be confused about when you feed each of them. You should also take note of the date each tarantula has moulted. With your record, you will be able to track the progress of the spider. It will also help to make a prediction on when a tarantula will moult. It will help you to know when fasting is as a result of preparation for moulting and when it is as a result of sickness.

Introducing Your Goliath Birdeater to their Home

Whether you purchased your pet tarantula or you caught it from the wild, you have to introduce it to its new home. Don't just drop the tarantula in the cage and lock it. The placement has to be properly and gently done for easy adaptation to the environment. When you receive your package, the box containing the tarantula in the cage; open it and turn the opening to its side gently. One end of the cage should be opposite the water dish. Leave the box and tarantula inside. Lock the cage. Don't disturb your giant tarantula. It will leave the box on its own and at a time that pleases it. Be checking it at intervals to know when it has exited the box. When it does, you can remove the box gently. It is not a good practice to remove the tarantula from the box forcefully.

You can only do that if you observe that leaving the box inside the cage will pose some danger to the tarantula or if the box is very large to be kept inside the cage. Just open the cage and turn the box so that the opening will be by the side. Get a plastic, glass or transparent drinking container, which you have to slide into the box over your GB to secure it inside. When it is inside the container and it is well secured, bring out the container and cover it. Then place the glass or plastic container inside the tarantula cage, remove the cover and bend it to the side. Leave the glass inside as instructed above for the giant tarantula to come out when it feels like it. If the tarantula does not leave the container, you don't have to bother it. Cover the cage and place it in the right location.

At this time, your newly arrived pet needs some rest and a moment of serenity. So, leave it alone to have some peace. At this point, don't bother providing the tarantula with food. Leave it for a couple of days without food. This is to allow it a few days to get accustomed to life in captivity within the cage. Don't worry, it will not die of starvation. Some beginners do wonder why the tarantula should not be given food when it is introduced to the cage for the first time. The reason is quite simple. There is the tendency for the spider to become frightened even by its prey because it has not become used to the new environment. This is why expert spider enthusiasts advise new keepers not to provide any feed to their tarantula when they are newly introduced to the cage, so that they will become used to life in the cage.

Chapter 5: Goliath Birdeater Caring Tips

The goliath birdeater is a special kind of animal that you keep at home. The way you care for it when it is held in captivity is quite different from the way you care for other wild animals that can be kept in captivity. This is because it is not only sensitive to temperature and humidity, it is temperamental and wild. It can never fall in love with its owner. So, if you are keeping such an animal, you should be very careful. In the preceding chapter, I have spent time talking about a spiderling and how it should be cared for. In this chapter, I am going to provide you with tips on how to care for your adult tarantula. I shall discuss its feeding, handling, the various ailments that can affect your tarantula and other topics of regarding its care.

Foods and Diet

The goliath birdeater is one of the easiest pets to take care of and feed. This is because it does not eat everyday and its foods are not difficult to get. Many people are deceived by the word "birdeaters" added to their names. The giant birdeaters may consume little birds, but even in the wild, they rarely hunt for birds. Rather, they feed more on invertebrates such as crickets and earthworms. Theraphosa blondi can also subdue and feed on mice, small lizards and small snakes.

While in captivity, you can feed them with the same food. What is important is the manner in which you provide your tarantulas with nourishment. Many beginners make the mistake of providing their giant killers with the same type of food regularly. But like human beings, tarantulas require variety. You need to vary their feed. The major types of foods to provide a goliath tarantula are live crickets, locusts, beetles, cockroaches, mealworms and earthworms. However, if you don't have live prey, you can serve dead food to your tarantula but live food is the best.

Mice or any other rodents should be sparingly provided because of the danger involved. You should ensure that your tarantula is big enough to kill a rodent. Although goliath birdeaters are really large and can kill a mouse, some rodents normally put up a fight before they are finally killed by tarantulas. The fight can be interesting to watch. But it is possible for the giant to sustain serious injury during the fight. So, to avoid such an ugly incidence, if you want to provide a mouse, it should be a small size that the spider can easily kill. Some expert keepers have also advised beginners to provide dead, frozen rodents, which have to be thawed before serving. Personally, I do provide little mice, which my giant birdeater has always subdued without sustaining any injury.

Another problem with feeding a tarantula with a mouse is that it can make the cage malodorous. This is because of the manner in which the mouse or lizard is consumed by the giant birdeater. Normally, a snake will swallow a mouse whole. But in the case of a tarantula, it does not consume it whole. Rather, it mashes it up before feeding. After feeding, the cage will be messed up, creating much more work for you to handle.

Feeding Dos and Don'ts

Whether you are serving live pinkie mice or insects, it is of crucial importance that you consider the size of your mice. The prey to be provided regardless of what it is should not be larger than the size of the abdomen of your tarantula. Ideally, one that is less than half the size of your tarantula will be ok.

Don't serve them with crickets or insects that are caught from the wild or around any farm treated with insecticides or pesticides. If you are going to serve your giant birdeater with prey caught in the wild, you have to be sure that the area where it is caught is free from pesticides or insecticides. In this way, you will eliminate the risk of exposing your pet to pesticides or insecticides. Note that some insecticides remain active for a long period in the body of an insect that consumes them and can even affect another predator that feeds on the insect as prey. So, if you if feed your tarantula with an insect that harbours an insecticide, it is likely to affect it and may result in its untimely death.

Fatten the insects before serving them. Just as human beings need nutritious foods to remain healthy, so does a tarantula. A prey is nutritious to the extent it is nurtured and fed. So, gut-load your prey and dust them with vitamins before feeding. In this way, your spider will obtain enough nutrients from their prey.

Provide your tarantula with a variety of prey. As already mentioned, it is not good to give your spider only one type of prey. Vary them for enhanced pleasure and a variety of nutrients.

The number of prey to serve per meal depends on the size of your pet and also on the size of the prey. One large insect may be enough to a tarantula of an average size. But if your tarantula is very large, you may serve two small prey. Give young giant birdeaters one prey at a time. But for adults, you can drop multiple live insects in its cage as it can handle them one after the other. Four or five crickets are enough in a week for an adult giant tarantula.

Feed them at night. In the wild, tarantulas normally hunt at night because they are nocturnal. It is therefore advisable to feed them at night.

Younger tarantulas should be fed more frequently than adults. In other words, the frequency of feeding depends on the age of the spider. Baby giant tarantulas should be fed, as I advised above, twice or thrice per week. For adults, you can provide them prey once or two times per week. Note that adult tarantulas can stay without food for up to a month. So, if everything, including the environment, is ok and your tarantula is not eating even though it is not preparing to moult, there is no cause for alarm. They don't eat when they don't feel like eating.

You can maintain a routine with the feeding. This means giving them food after every two or three days in a week depending on which ever option that you prefer. But some keepers don't maintain any routine. They want to replicate what happens in the wild. In the wild, giant birdeaters are not always successful in hunting for prey. They eat when they kill a prey. So, when they are not successful in killing a prey, they will fast. You may decide to feed your spider twice in a week and once in the following week and none in the other week. If you are following this pattern, there is no rule guiding the order. But make sure that you are not starving your tarantula.

How the Goliath Birdeater Feeds

To be a professional and experienced tarantula owner, you should also understand how tarantulas feed. The first point to bear in mind is that they don't feed in a conventional manner or like some conventional pets. They are stealthy killers. It lays ambush for the prey and once one appears in their way, it will immediately bounce on it, biting it with the fangs. It is also with the fangs that it will inject the venom in the prey. The venom will paralyse and kill the prey. As mentioned under the section on digestive system, tarantulas, in general, do not consume solid food. The prey will be transformed into a digestible liquid by the digestive enzymes. Now, it can start to feed by sucking up the liquid. Giant tarantulas do not require the web to kill but they can store food in the web in case they don't want it immediately.

Handling

Handling is a crucial issue in tarantula keeping. Some keepers will like to handle their spiders and take snapshots or make videos of themselves with their tarantulas on their palms. Indeed, this can be fun. But with goliath birdeaters, it should not be done. I have already talked about handling a giant tarantula spiderling. Here, I am going to talk about handling in general and why it is not good to handle a goliath birdeater.

There are several reasons why you should not handle a giant birdeater. First, it is a wild animal which cannot be tamed no matter how long it is held in captivity or how well it is treated. So, they cannot love you or differentiate you from another person. They lack the mental ability to differentiate between an intruder and an owner. Besides, their general attitude also makes it unwise to handle them. They are timid and always startled at little disturbance. It is better to leave them alone.

Apart from being skittish, they are somewhat aggressive, especially when they feel threatened. So, it is easy for a GB to misconceive handling as danger. When a tarantula is not feeling secure, it has to defend itself against the aggressor. The normal reaction is the release of the urticating bristle. Go back to chapter 1 to read about how the irritating hairs can affect you in a number of ways. You may be bitten as well. Refer to the chapter on tarantula bite to learn more about it, how to avoid being bitten and what to do when you are bitten.

Another reason why handling is discouraged is because of their size. An adult female goliath tarantula can be very large to the extent of covering both palms joined together. The fangs, which they use in biting, are commensurable to their body size. So, the larger a goliath birdeater is, the longer the fangs will be. The fangs of some larger species are up to an inch in length, which can create deep wounds in their prey or aggressor when they bite. You can imagine how painful it will be if a fang of such length goes deep inside your body.

Another important point to consider regarding the size of a tarantula as far as handling is concerned is the possibility of falls. Spiders in general do not have a hard exoskeleton like ants. They are plump and a drop from any height can be deadly. The abdomen is very large and when it hits the ground from it will be as if a nylon filled with water is dropped. There will be a blast. Don't think a fall will not happen. You can, as a result of fear, drop the spider on the ground. Such falls can result in the rupture of the abdomen or in a broken limb.

As I advised above in the section on the handling of spiderling, I will also suggest that you use an artist brush to corral a straying adult goliath tarantula. You can also apply the method mentioned in the same section to bring in or send out a giant tarantula from a cage. In this way, you will eliminate any possibility of abdominal rupture.

Ailment of a Goliath Birdeater

Like every other living thing, a goliath birdeater can fall sick and die. But it is affected by just a few illnesses to the extent that is known to the researchers today. As a keeper, sometimes my goliath birdeater does fall sick. My major challenge whenever my spider is having a health challenge is being able to determine what is wrong with it. They are not like other conventional pets that you can take to a veterinarian. However, based on experience, I am going to tell you some of the illnesses that tarantulas normally have.

Dehydration

Dehydration is one of the health conditions that have killed a lot of goliath birdeaters when they are held in captivity. One of the reasons why these invertebrates suffer from this condition is because they are not properly provided with sufficient water and their environment is not sufficiently humid. Though these species of spiders obtain moisture from their prey, they need to stay in an environment that is sufficiently moist as they also get their water from the condensation by the corners of their cage and from the water dish provided for them. For adults, you have to also provide them with water dishes so that when they are in need of water, they will find water to drink.

Many novice keepers think that the giant tarantulas have no need for water. They do drink water, and if they are not given it, this can kill them. There are some symptoms that show when your tarantula is suffering from dehydration. If the body of your tarantula becomes wrinkled, it is likely that it is suffering from dehydration. A dehydrated tarantula also looks shrunken or shrivelled. The spider will be lethargic.

When you observe such symptoms, you don't need to be told what to do. Your spider does not require any other medication except water. Provide it with water as instructed above. Then check the substrate to ensure that it is sufficiently moist. This will help to relieve the symptoms and hydrate the spider quickly. Note that if you don't take appropriate action, the spider is likely going to die.

Mould and Fungi Infection
The effort to maintain a humid environment for a tarantula birdeater can go wrong; creating a favourable environment for fungi like mould and mildew to develop in the living space of the spider. The development of mould, mildew and other kinds of fungi in a giant birdeater's cage is never without consequences. Just as human beings can develop certain fungi infection when they are exposed to an environment where these microorganisms are, so will tarantulas. Important internal organs can be affected by fungi if they are living in an infected environment. The infection will show itself through some symptoms. If your tarantula pet is suffering from fungi infection, watch out for uneven spots of cream colour on different parts of the tarantula such as the tips of the legs, abdomen or carapace. Fungi infection, especially one that is in an advanced stage, is very difficult to handle. Thus, it is advisable that you do everything possible to prevent it rather than allowing it to occur. But when it occurs, there are certain treatments to give your spider. Apply betadine to the affected area. But you should be very careful here, as you may have to handle the spider.

Remember what was said on how to avoid getting bitten by a tarantula. You have to move your tarantula pet to a well ventilated and clean cage with the required humidity and temperature. Normally, fungi die if they are exposed to an environment that is not favourable to them. They don't like an airy environment. If the infection is very serious, you may consider immersing your pet in a solution that is about 10% alcoholic. This treatment should be provided as a last option.

Parasites

Parasites are always a problem for spider enthusiasts. This is because of lack of treatment for the type of parasites and pests that affect invertebrates like spiders and others. You cannot give tarantulas insecticides or pesticides as a means of killing the parasites. If you do, you may end up killing your spider. This is why you should make every effort to protect your giant birdeater from a parasite infection. The best way to achieve that is by maintaining a good environment and keeping your pet's dwelling place very neat.

Tarantulas can be affected by both internal and external parasites. A typical example of internal parasites that have a terrible effect on Goliath birdeaters are nematodes. A tarantula affected by nematodes normally looks sick. It does not feed well. The tarantula is also restless. It will also cause the spider to produce a lot of silk. Another symptom manifested by an infected tarantula is that it stays more in the water dish. The cage will also have sickly sweet smell. Take a look at the mouth area of the spider to see if you will find a white, gummy mass of goo. If you find any, it is a clear indication that your pet is internally infected with nematodes. For now, no remedy has been discovered but research is ongoing in this regard. So, there is not much you can do for a tarantula infected by nematodes except to keep taking care of it until it takes its last breath. You should also consider sending it to any research institute within your locality that may be interested in using the spider for research purposes.

Externally, mites can invade the cage of a tarantula. If your tarantula is infected with mites, you will know, as they are visible to the naked eye. Normally, they occupy the mouth area of the host. They may not cause serious symptoms. However, they can constitute serious disturbances to the tarantula, which will cause them stress. Stress can make the tarantula not feed very well and this can affect its general well being. Mites are tiny and can find their way into the book lungs and oral hole of the tarantula, especially when they are present in large numbers. When this happens, the death of your spider is imminent.

The species of mites that is commonly found in a spider cage is the house dust mite, known to scientists as Glycyphagus domesticus. The reason why they are normally seen in a tarantula cage is quite obvious. This is because they are almost present in every house, including houses of those that do not keep pets like spiders. Many keepers blame breeders when their giant tarantulas are infested. But experience has shown that live-food breeders are innocent in most cases. House dust mites thrive well in an environment similar to the one that tarantulas prefer. Since these mites are normally available in the homes, they will definitely find themselves inside the cage of your pet spider, which has a favourable environment for their survival.

When they enter the cage, they will relax there as the environment favours their survival and there are also foods to consume if your cage is dirty. These tiny parasites feed on decaying organic matter. Thus, if you don't keep the cage clean and remove leftover food, then you are inviting them for a scrumptious meal.

Bear in mind that it is almost impossible to prevent these tiny creatures from entering into your tarantula cage, given the reason mentioned above. However, on the positive side, it is not difficult to control them. Besides, when they are available in small numbers, they will be of no negative consequence. Instead, they will help to sanitise your cage as they feed on food remnants that you could not remove or you did not see.

Apart from the house dust mites, another species of mites can invade the cage of Pterinochilus affinis, which is another species of tarantula that I keep. I have observed that these species normally reside around the mouth region of this tarantula. But it is also possible to find some around other parts of the body of the species. However, there are things about these mites that I have no information on. First, I am not sure whether or not they can affect goliath birdeaters, as I have not actually found them in any of my giant tarantulas. But I assume that they can since all tarantulas have a similar nature. Secondly, I cannot tell with certainty what effect these species of mites have on their hosts because I have only noticed them just in a cage. But I think they don't cause any problem to the pet if they are available in small numbers. Furthermore, I also have no information about their source of nourishment. I am not sure whether they feed on the tarantula's leftover or on the blood of the tarantula.

If you observe any species of mites on your pet tarantula, you should make an effort to remove them. Use an artist brush to sweep them out. Apply some Vaseline on the brush. Gently and lightly pat it on the goliath birdeater as you remove the mites. The spider may feel threatened and become defensive. So, you should put on the necessary gear. Be careful to avoid being bitten by the tarantula. Note that mites don't easily die. You need to pop them open using your thumb-nails. You can also rake them together using the brush and then use the trowel to remove them from the cage. Burn them to kill them or apply a suitable pesticide on them.

Don't put an infected tarantula to mate with an uninfected spider. This is because it is a veritable means of spreading these parasites. During mating the mites will disperse and some will move to the uninfected as they run for safety. Goliath birdeaters make noise during mating and this can frighten the mites making them run for safety. So, it is important that you ensure that each of the mating partners have no mites.

Before you make use of any old terrarium, cage or aquarium as a home for your pet tarantula, regardless of the material it is made from, I will advise you to first apply disinfectants on it. If there are mites or maggots of small flies still on the cage, it will kill them. You should also spray all decorative items, including trees in the cage, with the disinfectant, as these tiny insects and parasites can hide on these items.

Wounds and damage to body tissues

As already mentioned above, tarantula birdeaters are very large and chubby. Thus it is easy for them to sustain injuries or break their limbs when they fall. They are burrowers and not good climbers. So, they may fall down in an attempt to escape from their cage. This is why it is important that I mention it here, even though in the strict sense of it injuries, wounds and damaged tissues are not illnesses or diseases. If a tarantula survives the injuries, the wounded part will be regenerated during the next moulting.

Note that despite the ability of GBs to regenerate damaged tissues or parts during moulting, wounds can cause the death of a spider. This is because their blood is not the type that coagulates. This means that no scab will be formed on any wound and this can have a devastating effect on the spider. To this effect, the best thing to do is to help the giant birdeater not to have any wounds at all. There are a number of things that you can do in order to prevent falls that will lead to injury of the spider. Make sure that there is no sharp object on the cage. Use the right material for the substrate.

Virtually all the materials mentioned above are not very hard and so falls on such substrate will not result to serious injury. Tarantula birdeaters are terrestrial, or burrowers, and thus they will not require any trees. So, you save them from the temptation of climbing by not including any tree or similar items. This doesn't mean that they will not attempt to climb. Their prey may climb and they can climb up in pursuit of the prey without knowing the consequence of what they are doing. Also keep them in a low walled cage as instructed above so that even if they climb the walls and fall, the impact will not be heavy. Wounds can be treated or first aid treatment can be given. I am going to discuss this in a separate subheading in this chapter.

In summary, I can say that tarantulas in general are susceptible to only a few illnesses, which can be avoided if you do what is necessary or if you follow the tips given here. The key to maintaining a healthy tarantula is keeping up with good cage hygiene.

Note that a tarantula will be on its back during moulting. This is not a symptom of any sickness.

Giving First Aid Treatment to Your Goliath Birdeater

As evident from the above, goliath tarantulas can suffer from few illnesses. Fortunately, they rarely become sick. But unfortunately, there are just a few exotic vets that are willing to treat a sick tarantula. So, it may be that your tarantula solely depends on you in order to get well. Given this, it is of crucial importance that you learn how to administer first aid treatment to a sick tarantula. Here, I am going to teach you how to give first aid treatment to a sick tarantula.

Establish your tarantula intensive care unit

Does it sound strange to you? Indeed, this is the first thing that you should do. Therefore, you must learn how to create an ICU for your tarantula. It is not a big deal and does not require any hospital equipment. You only need to get a plastic dish or a deli cup that has enough room to accommodate your spider. Create tiny holes by the side of the container for air circulation. Get some pieces of towel and dampen them with water. Pack them very well and neatly. Place them at the bottom of the deli cup to provide a soft and calming effect on your tarantula. Provide a small dish of water in the ICU. I recommend that you place the container close to a humidifier as a means of maintaining the humidity level within the dish. But if you don't have a humidifier, you can do without this even though it is highly recommended.

The ICU will be helpful to you when dealing with certain illnesses. With this set up, you can handle dehydration issues. Just put the dehydrated goliath birdeater in the deli cup prepared as instructed above. Bring the water dish close to the spider's mouth. Tarantulas do not breathe from the mouth, rather, they use their book lungs to breathe. They are located under the side of their abdomens. So, you may also place the mouth of your tarantula in the water. It will not die of suffocation. But don't keep the abdomen inside the water dish as this may affect its breathing. Leave it inside the ICU for 12 hours but be checking on it occasionally. If you get this right, your tarantula will get relief and its conditions will improve within a day.

You can also make use of the ICU in handling bad or wet moult as well as injury that causes fluid leak. Bad or wet moult rarely occurs. There is no scientific explanation to that. The healthiest spider can even experience that. If it happens to your spider, all you need to do is to move it to the ICU as instructed above. Your tarantula at this time requires much intake of water in order to replace the fluid going out of the body. So, if you keep its mouth close to the water dish so that it will access water, it will be of help to it. The same goes for injury that leads to loss of fluid.

Injury first aid treatment

The best way to treat injury is to avoid it. As I have mentioned above, injury in tarantulas does not form scabs because it does not have blood in the real sense of it. I have always done everything possible to ensure that my GB does not have any injuries. But I am going to share some of the tips I learnt from other expert keepers on how to treat a tarantula. I have tried just one and it worked. Here are injury treatment tips to try.

First aid with toilet paper

Place toilet tissue paper on any bleeding part of the GB. Leave it there to stick to the part as it mixes with the hemolynph. It will turn into a band aid. It will remain in the part till the next moult when regeneration will take place. The toilet paper will be moulted out.

Try Talcum

Apply talcum on the injured part. This will help to stop the bleeding. Avoid the book lungs when applying the talcum, as it is the breathing organ. If it comes in contact with the book lungs, it means that it will enter the GB's lung and this is not good for its health.

Stanch bleeding with Vaseline

Apply a petroleum jelly Vaseline on the wound, as it will help in stopping bleeding.

Invest in liquid bandages

Liquid bandages are very effective in the treatment of wounds in tarantulas, as it can stop bleeding quickly. However, the problem with this method is its cost. It is available at a very high price tag. But if you can afford one, it is worth buying. Besides, they are not readily available on the market. On the positive side, it is very easy to be used. A drop on the wounded part is enough to stop bleeding.

Be a surgeon

If a limb is badly damaged such that amputating it is a better option, you have no other option than to play the surgeon. Get a dental wire or any other suitable alternative. Tie it on the injured limb just on a segment above the wound in order to stop the flow of hemolynph. Then cut off the wounded part with a pair of scissors. The tarantula will manage until the next moulting when a new limb will replace the damaged one.

Making use of super glue or enamel for nails

This should be sparingly used or should be used as a last resort because these products are strong.

The method to be used depends on the degree of injury. I will recommend that use the first two methods, toilet paper and talcum first. This is because they don't contain any chemicals like the rest of the solutions. But you can try other methods, if the conditions do not improve. Regardless of the method you are using, you have to be very careful in applying it. Tarantula limbs are not like that those of the conventional pets. So, use a paintbrush to apply any of these solutions when necessary.

Catching an Escaped Goliath Birdeater

Giant tarantulas and indeed all spiders are skilful opportunists. A tarantula will always escape from a cage once it finds an opportunity, regardless of how long it has been inside the cage. If a tarantula escapes captivity, you have to do everything possible to get it back because her presence outside the cage is not a good thing both for the spider and your household. It can bite somebody. But the spider can also become a good meal for some of its predators such as big lizards and birds. People within the neighbours can kill it. The spider may also expose itself to the household chemicals. You can see why it is important for you to do everything possible to find an escaped tarantula.

Delay may be dangerous

Immediately when you observe that your tarantula has escaped from the cage, you need to look for it. The first line of action to take is to lock the entrance to the room where the tarantula cage is. In this way, you will forestall the possibility of the spider leaving the room. You should not forget to close the windows and any opening that leads outside the room.

Put the household on alert

Now, you have to let everybody know so that they will be careful and alert until the spider is found. This reduces the possibility of any person stamping on the tarantula or the possibility of the spider biting any member of your family in self-defence. The next thing you have to do is to put all your pets, if you have any, in their cage, which will be kept in a room where you are sure the tarantula is not in. Now everybody seems to be safe, you can now start the search for the escaped spider.

Searching for an escaped tarantula

It is important to search very well. But there are some spots that the spider is likely to hide. You have to search such places, which include edges of the container (tanks), corners of the walls of the room, around and under any furniture in the room. If you cannot find it in and around of these spots mentioned in the room where the cage is, then you have to search the entire house. Pay more attention to more humid and dark areas in the house such as under the sink, bathroom or behind the heater. Tarantula birdeaters do not climb and so no need looking on high places. But if it is an arboreal species that you keep, then you have to look for it in high places.

Contacting your neighbours

After searching you entire house and compound, if you don't see it, then you have to let your neighbours know so that they will be very careful in their homes and also help you to look for it. You should also allay their fears by explaining to them that tarantula birdeaters are big but not harmful. But also warn them about their urticating bristles, the noise they make when they feel threaten and the possibility of the spider biting a conceived aggressor. Tell them to call you if they find it. Rather than picking it up by themselves, they should cover it with a container so that you can collect it by yourself. Let the animal control unit of your locality know about your missing tarantula if you cannot find it.

Picking up an escaped tarantula

Once it is found, try to overcome the temptation of being in a hurry to pick it up. Remember that it is not a dog that will embrace you. It does not know you. Make sure that you put on your gloves. Use an artist brush to gently brush it into a container and take it back to its cage. However, if you don't have an artist brush, you may still be able to pick up your pet tarantula with your hand. The words to bear in mind if you are to go by this option are "gently and carefully." These creatures are very fragile. Their limbs can easily be broken if little pressure is applied to them. The swollen abdomen can rupture if they are grabbed with force. You can see why you should be gentle and careful when handling your tarantula.

There are some tricks to apply to gently pick up a strayed pet spider. Put on your garden gloves. Gently place your palm in front of the tarantula in such a manner that it will not be frightened and apprehensive. The tarantula will crawl on your palm. If it refuses to climb on your palm, just give it a little tap on the abdomen. Take it inside and place it back in its cage. You can also pick up the tarantula but you have to hold it between the middle legs, that is, at the joining point between the head region and abdomen. But don't hold it on the abdomen to prevent any possibility of popping it open. Note that no matter how gentle you are when picking up your tarantula, it will release the urticating hairs on you. This is why you should make use of the gloves.

But you need to be careful and prevent future occurrences. The best way to do that is to ensure that the cage is covered with a tight fitting lid. Note that a tarantula is very big and its weight alone can lift open a lid. So, I suggest that you place a heavy item on the cage to weight the cover down. You can also tie the lid. In this way, you will frustrate the pet's attempt to escape captivity. Another means of preventing the tarantula from escaping is to cage it with a well made cage. Refer to the chapter on housing requirements.

Signs that Your Tarantula Will Bite

Goliath tarantulas are mildly aggressive. Like other aggressive species, they are calm when they are not messed with and are not apprehensive of anything. But when disturbed or when they feel threatened, they will react, release their urticating hairs and bite. But before they bite, they will always show signs that they will bite. It will move back on the hind legs showing its fangs as a warning to the perceived aggressor that it can bite. But in most cases, it will not bite. It will only fling the bristles. It does not want to waste the venom as it uses it to kill prey. So, it turns around to show the abdomen, it is a sign that it will release the hairs if you continue disturbing it. But if the aggressor is not scared, the spider has no option than to bite. Sometimes, tarantulas bite without injecting the venom. The bite is not to kill but to scare.

Chapter 6: A Look at a Goliath Birdeater's Bite

As I have already mentioned above, tarantulas in general and even other species of spiders don't ordinarily bite human beings, like ants and some other insects. They only bite humans when they are threatened or for defence purposes. In the course of taking care of your tarantula, you may be bitten by the animal you are feeding. This should not be a surprise to you because the spider does not see you as a friend. But if you are bitten, what are you going to do? Is the bite painful? Is it deadly? What first aid treatment will you give yourself? How dangerous is the bite? Do you need to schedule an appointment with a doctor? These and some other concerns are what I will be discussing in this chapter.

How to Avoid Getting Bitten

Goliath birdeaters have fangs for burrowing and killing prey. But it can also use the fangs to bite when it is threatened. As it is said in the medical parlance, prevention is better than cure. If you don't want to suffer from itching skin and pain resulting from spider's bite, then you have to forestall any possibility of the spider biting you. You cannot stop the animal from biting you just by training it, as it cannot be trained. You only have to be careful and apply the necessary tips given below.

Put on the necessary gear when handling your goliath tarantula or when you are working on its cage. Wear a pair of gloves and wear long pants, which should be tucked into your boots. Also put on a long-sleeved shirt. It can be tiresome and boring putting all these on just to attend to your spider. But the truth is that it is worth doing if you don't want to risk being bitten. Apart from protecting you from being bitten, these clothes will also protect you from the urticating bristle of the spider, which it will release when it is threatened.

Leave your giant birdeater alone. As already mentioned above, tarantulas as well as other species of spiders don't bite unless they feel threatened or disturbed. So, if you only provide your spider with its nourishment and leave it, then it will not bite you. As I have suggested above, use transparent containers if you will like to be seeing your tarantula kill and consume its prey.

Cover the cage. Your spider will not escape if their cage is covered properly. This will reduce the chance of the tarantula escaping and entering inside a living room which when it happens will expose your children to risk of being bitten.

What Does a Tarantula Bite Look and Feel Like?

Tarantula bites can be differentiated from the bite of other insects both in their pain and look. So, if you feel that you are bitten but you are not very sure, the look and feel of the bite will tell you whether or not you have been bitten by a tarantula. Have you been stung by a bee before? If the answer to the question is yes, then you will not have any problem identifying a spider's bite. This is because the pain of tarantula bites is very much similar to the pain of a bee sting. The spot where you are bitten will redden. It will also swell. Though the venom is weak and cannot kill a human being, the reaction of the bite can go beyond the spot where you are bitten to other parts of the body.

First Aid Treatment When Bitten

The first thing to do is wash the bite with cool water and soap in order to forestall the possibility of the area becoming infected before you can see a doctor, if there is a need for that.

Cool the bite spot by applying a cool compress over it. You can place an ice pack or place a piece of cloth soaked in cold water on the spot. This will help to ease the pain of the bite. If the pain has become too much or unbearable, you can take a pain relief medication to relieve it.

Tie a snug bandage above the bite. You can also elevate the limb if you are bitten on the leg or arm. Move as little as you can. Doing these will help to stop the venom from spreading quickly. It will also help to reduce inflammation and swelling. Don't tight-tie the bandage at the bitten spot in such a manner that blood circulation to the area is inhibited.

If your child is the one bitten and he or she has symptoms of flu or is recovering from chickenpox, you have to administer aspirin to the child.

Keep an eye on the bite. Even though goliath birdeaters' venom are not deadly, it is of crucial importance that you monitor the bite throughout the day.

When to see a doctor

Seeing a doctor if you are bitten by a tarantula may not be necessary due to the weakness of the venom. Experienced keepers are used to the bite and not all will result in a hospital visit. So, monitor the bitten area. If the pain becomes too much or spreads to other parts of the body producing redness and swelling, you have to see a doctor. Alternatively, you can ring the emergency medical services. Other symptoms that should result in a hospital visit include the following:

- difficult breathing
- feeling faint
- profuse sweating
- the spread of stripy pattern from the bite spot
- muscle spasms
- tightening in the throat, which makes swallowing difficult

Your doctor will give you some antibiotics. Depending on the severity of the symptoms, the doctor can also prescribe certain medical tests to determine whether or not the venom still remains in your bloodstream.

Note that tarantulas have no anti-venoms. This is because the bite is not of serious consequence. The venom is weak. So, if you go to a doctor, only antibiotics such as Benadryl will be administered to you and the doctor will charge you for his time.

There are some people that have contemplated removing the fangs of their tarantula to prevent it from biting. This is never a solution to prevent a tarantula bite. It will only facilitate the death of your tarantula. When you remove the fang, the spider will no longer eat and will not be able to kill any prey. But it will grow another one during the next moulting. That will only happen if it does not die of starvation. Such also makes it vulnerable to the attack of some insects, including its prey. This is because the fangs are like tarantula jaws. Imagine what will happen to you if your jaws are removed. The pain alone will be enough to kill you. Just as a lion is powerless if it has no jaw so is a tarantula powerless if it has no fang.

Chapter 7: Moulting in Goliath Birdeaters

I have briefly discussed moulting as a growth process in spiderling. But it is an important biological occurrence and deserves a thorough examination. Besides, it is not only baby goliath tarantulas that undergo it. Adult giant birdeaters also go through this process. It is a natural process and through it the tarantula regenerates a damaged limb. Tarantulas benefit a lot from the process but it also makes them weak and exposes them to danger. For a tarantula to survive all this important growth process, you need to get it right. The care given to a tarantula that prepares for or that is moulting is not the same with the care given to one that is not moulting. In this chapter, I am going to examine moulting in details and provide you with tips on how to handle your goliath birdeater as it undergoes this important life process.

What Is Moulting?

Moulting, as mentioned above, is a natural process through which a tarantula shades its exoskeleton and develops a new one. It is a growth process because through its occurrence a spiderling continues its growth into adult stage. Damaged tissues and broken limbs are also regenerated during moulting. The process is not just strenuous and stressful but also painful and difficult for tarantulas undergoing it. It makes it a prey to its prey.

Tarantulas prepare for this process before undergoing it. The spider will stop eating and may lose the abdominal hairs. It will take a giant birdeater about fifteen hours to complete the moulting process. But it does not need any disturbance throughout the entire period of the development. At the completion of the process, your pet tarantula will look very fragile, soft, tender and sensitive. It is not a time to touch it or disturb it. Allow it a couple of days to develop a strong exoskeleton to be able to live a normal life and also to be able to take on a prey.

Note that the limbs or tissues regenerated during moulting are not immediately as useful as the old ones. They are normally shorter and will take some time to grow into fully fledged limbs.

Moulting Signs

As already mentioned, tarantulas prepare for moulting and they exhibit some signs to show that they are preparing for it. It is important that you know these signs so that when your pet tarantula begins to exhibit them, you will know the right line of action to take.

Abstinence from food

Normally, a tarantula preparing for moulting will stop eating. I cannot actually tell why spiders will fast in preparation for such a painful exercise. I have not come across any scientific explanation for that. I will only assume that it is a natural defensive mechanism. As moulting day is drawing near, they are becoming weaker and weaker. So, if they continue eating, they may turn out to be good meal for their prey. If you observe that your spider has stopped eating or has not eaten the food provided, check their environmental conditions. If all conditions are ok with your spider, it is most likely that the lack of interest in food is because it is preparing for moulting. However, don't conclude with just one meal. The fasting normally lasts for days or even up to a week. So, if it does not eat a meal, provide another to see if it will consume it. If the lack of interest for food persists for days, your pet tarantula must be preparing for moulting.

Darkening abdomen

Many older or young adult goliath birdeaters, as well as those of other species of tarantulas, have bald spots on their abdomens. The defensive urticating hairs are located on these spots. But as the spider releases these irritating bristles towards a preconceived threat in self-defence, the spot gradually becomes bald. When a tarantula birdeater is preparing for moulting, this bald spot on the abdomen will become darker in colour. The darkening of the spot is because of the development of a new exoskeleton under the old one. Thus, it is a surer sign that your pet tarantula fasting from food is preparing to moult. However, you cannot rely on this sign if your spider does not have any bald patches. This is because the bristle will not allow you to see the darkened abdomen clearly.

Enlarged abdomen

I have mentioned earlier that moulting is a growth process. When a baby tarantula needs to grow, it has to moult. Before the moulting occurs, signs of growth will also show. An enlarged or swollen abdomen is one of such signs. If you notice that the abdomen of your pet tarantula has swollen and looks as if it is going to burst open, you may assume that the spider is about to moult. However, this sign is not reliable and not a scientific method when it comes to an adult tarantula. This is because there are other factors that can cause an adult giant tarantula to have a swollen abdomen. The abdomen of spiders in general expands like a sack and so when they eat, it will also become enlarged and looks as if it wants to pop open. So, you have to use this sign together with other signs.

Weak and lazy in behaviour

Goliath birdeaters, during the preparatory stage for moulting, become lazy and almost inactive. They rarely move and may remain in a corner. This is because of the high energy and effort required for the development of the new skin underneath the old one that will be shaded. If you notice that your tarantula has suddenly become sluggish and prefers staying in one place, chances are that it is preparing for moulting. However, the spider should also exhibit other signs before you can conclude that it is about to moult. This is because inactivity or sluggishness can also be as a result of other serious health conditions.

More silk production

A tarantula becomes a toothless bulldog during and few days after moulting. It can be killed by an insect that was once its prey. However, since it is a natural process, Mother Nature also has a way of protecting them from predator. During this time, tarantulas in the wild make more silk to cover their burrows to prevent intruders from entering inside. This attitude is common among Cobalt Blue or Green Bottle Blue as well as species of tarantulas that naturally produce a large amount of silk for webbing.

The occurrence of each of these signs is not sufficient to conclude that a spider is about to moult. If you notice any of them, don't assume that your pet tarantula is about to moult. You should also look for the other signs. A more reliable conclusion is drawn when the spider exhibit multiple signs.

Now that you know the various signs that are indicative of moulting, it is now time to tell you what you should do when it is evidently clear that your pet tarantula is preparing for moulting.

Taking Care of a Moulting Tarantula

Moulting, as I have mentioned above, is a highly delicate process. Many beginners have reported losing their pet tarantulas during this period because they did not do what they are supposed to do or as a result of negligence. Get it right, your spider will grow and become stronger but get it wrong, you put the life of your pet into jeopardy. It may die. Here are the right things to do in order to ensure that nothing happens to your giant birdeater during this stressful period.

No more food

Once you notice that your goliath tarantula has started fasting or abstaining from food in preparation for moulting, stop providing it with food. Many beginners have the fear that their tarantulas will die of starvation. You don't need to have such fear. Nothing will happen to your pet because the fasting is as a result of a natural process. Besides, even if you give the animal some food, it will not consume it. You are only putting its life into jeopardy because the live crickets moving about can get the tarantula agitated and fighting may ensue. The tarantula is weak and may not survive the fight. So, the rule of thumb is no more food until few days after moulting.

Provide a hideout for the tarantula

If you don't have any hideout in your cage, it will be good that you add one to your tarantula's cage during this time. This is because tarantulas do not like disturbance as they moult. They prefer staying in a hidden location and moult in a private area. The hide will be a perfect location for moulting for the spider.

Make the environment damper

Damp environment aids moulting. Experience has shown that if the environment is dry during this period, the tarantula will have to pass through difficult times in order to moult. Sometimes, it may not survive it. Consequently, to ease the pain and stress of moulting, it is advisable you increase the humidity level of your pet's living environment. This is not a difficult task to achieve. All you need to do is to spray water on the substrate to increase its moisture content. You may also have to spray tepid water on the cage or container. However, you don't have to overdo this. The substrate should not be soaked otherwise you make the atmosphere inside the cage favourable for the survival of fungi.

Don't disturb the tarantula

The moulting period is not a time to display your tarantula or show it to your visitors. It is a period to give your tarantula privacy and a serene atmosphere free from any disturbance. On no account should you handle your tarantula during this period. In order to ensure that they have absolute privacy, you should clean up the cage and remove unconsumed foods when you are sure it is preparing for moulting. In this way, you will not have to bother them again with anything.

Signs that a Tarantula Has Successfully Moulted

After the preparatory stage and if everything goes smoothly, your tarantula will moult successfully. But the preparatory stage may last for weeks. The problem first time keepers normally have is being able to tell that your tarantula has successfully moulted. There are also some signs exhibited by the spider that will let you know. Here are signs that moulting has taken place successfully.

The presence of slough

The most reliable sign that a tarantula has successfully moulted is the presence of slough in the cage. The shaded skin may look like a real and live spider. There are stories of beginners that confused this with their goliath spider. You should be able to differentiate this from the real exoskeleton. It all depends on where the moulting takes place. You may not see the slough immediately if the shading of the exoskeleton takes places within the hole or in a hidden corner. So, if you have not seen the slough, don't draw a hasty conclusion that the spider has not moulted.

Regular stretching

Tarantulas get fit after moulting. They normally stretch their limbs and push fluid through them. The stretching helps the new limbs to become strong and reach its full length. So, if you observe your pet stretching the limbs more often than usual, it is likely that it has completed moulting successfully.

Sitting in odd positions

Tarantulas put up some odd behaviour after moulting and one of them is sitting in odd positions. So, observe your Theraphosa blondi very well. Compare its behaviour now with how it was behaving previously. If you notice that the spider has begun to sit in an odd position, it might be that it has completed moulting. Normally, it will sit casually by the sides. But at the completion of moulting, it stretches out its legs in front and behind as if they are performing yoga or a stretching exercise.

Change in colour

During preparation for moulting, a tarantula will become darker in colour. But after moulting the colour will change and become more amazing and brighter. The colour change that occurs after moulting is the most reliable and convincing sign that a tarantula has completed its moulting. The bristle on the body will be smoother and silkier. The bald spot on the abdomen will disappear because the hairs are now new and none have been released. The look of the giant birdeater after moulting is a nice sight to behold. It will look very fragile and bright.

If your tarantula was younger before moulting, it will appear like an adult after the completion of the process. This means that it has the colour of an adult. Recall what has been said above on moulting in general. It is a growth process through which a juvenile tarantula grows into an adult. So, if you notice that your baby tarantula's colour is like that of an adult tarantula, there is no other explanation except that it has completed its moulting.

More active

Remember that during the preparatory stage, your tarantula was sluggish as it gathers energy for moulting. But after moulting, it will gradually go about its normal business and become more active. Days after moulting, the exoskeleton will become stronger. The spider has its fangs back and it can engage a prey in a fight. So, it will become more active. Besides, many days of fasting will make the pet tarantula become hungry. It has no other option than to wander about in search of food.

If the tarantula was inside the hole or in a hideout during the period of moulting and you have not seen it for sometimes, it will come out of the hole or hiding. You can see it now when you peep inside the cage. You will assume that it has completed moult successfully.

It is now time to provide the animal with food. However, the occurrence of one sign is not enough to conclude that moulting has taken place successfully. It is better to observe multiple signs before concluding that the process has been completed successfully.

Life after Moulting

Anytime my tarantula has moulted successfully, I normally experience a feeling of happiness that follows a great accomplishment. You will feel the same way when you observe that tarantula has completed moulting successfully. Your spiderling, with the completion of moulting has become more active, brighter and bigger. But this is not the time to rest and fan yourself that you have to done. There are things you should do to ensure that the tarantula continues with its normal life without any problems. Here are what to do after moulting.

Nourishment

Don't provide food immediately. The organs of attack like the fangs as well as the limbs and other organs have not fully become strong and developed. So, you have to give the tarantula a couple of days or a week so that these organs will fully develop and become functional as normal. Just introduce one feeder cricket in the cage after this period and watch what goes on between it and the spider. The tarantula will not waste any time in attacking it because it must be hungry by now. You can now introduce the second one depending on the number of prey you have been providing. Continue feeding in the usual manner or as instructed above.

Cleaning the cage

When the tarantula is back to its feet and going about its normal life, you have to clean up the cage. You don't have to leave the slough in the cage otherwise you create room for unwanted parasites and microorganisms to develop in the cage to feed on it. At this time, the tarantula will be aggressive. It has not shaded its aggressive nature. So, be careful as you remove the slough. Use a long pair of metal forceps to scrape it from the cage.

Sexing time

If you don't know the sex of your tarantula, this is the time to do it. Don't tear the slough into pieces. By now, you should know how to go about it. Refer to the section on sexing to know what to do. Why is sexing important? Sexing is indeed very important, especially for those planning to continue in tarantula husbandry by breeding their own goliath birdeater. Remember what was said about the lifespan of tarantulas. The male has a short lifespan. So, if you don't know their sex, you will not know when a male tarantula has matured.

Keep records of the moulting dates

I have already mentioned above why you should keep record of moulting dates. The only thing that I would want to add is that it will help you to know when your tarantula has become an adult. This is because younger tarantulas moult more frequently as they require it for growth. But adults normally moult once per year and almost always at the same time. So, if your tarantula begins to moult less frequently or once in year, it is a sign that it has become an adult. This brings us to one of the frequently asked question by beginners in many forums that I belong to. That is 'how many times does a tarantula moult in a life time?' Moulting is a natural process that continues till death. It occurs more often in spiderling than in adults.

So, it is difficult to tell how many times a goliath tarantula will shade its exoskeleton before dying. However, bear in mind that adult females will moult more than the males because they have a longer lifespan. After maturity, a male may have the opportunity to moult only once more. In the case of baby goliath birdeaters, the rate or frequency at which they moult depends to a greater extent on how much they eat. The more you feed a juvenile tarantula, the more frequently it will moult. But generally speaking, they moult once a month or once in two months.

Moulting FAQ

Here are some of the questions that beginners frequently asked about moulting that may be of interest to you.

How long does the moulting process last?

Unlike the preparatory stage for moulting, which takes days or weeks to be completed, the actual moulting process does not take a long time. It can be completed within half an hour or a couple of hours. However, it will take days for a new exoskeleton to become stiff so that the tarantula will continue its normal life.

At what time of the day does moulting occur?

Moulting can occur at any time of the day. All that the spider requires to moult is the needed privacy. However, most giant tarantulas I have kept normally moult at night or during the early morning hours. This is because tarantulas are nocturnal in nature.

How does a tarantula moult?

When a tarantula birdeater, or any other species of tarantula, is moulting, it lies on its back (there are some species that will lie by the sides). So, if you see your tarantula lying on its back, it is not ill or dead. If it is dead, its legs are more likely to be tucked inside them. So, you should not touch your pet if it is lying on its back. It is fragile at this time because it is undergoing a stressful process of their life.

Chapter 8: General Information about the Goliath Birdeater

The tips given in the preceding chapters are enough for you to get started with. However, there are some nitty-gritty and helpful hints that do not fit into any of the chapters and I think they will be useful to you as a beginner in tarantula keeping. In this chapter, I will discuss them one after the other so that you will be knowledgeable enough to keep a goliath tarantula captive in your home.

Things to Do and Things to Avoid

Goliath tarantulas are solitary animals. They can be regarded as territorial cannibals. One can kill the other. So, if you want to keep more than one giant birdeater, you should make provisions for two cages or provide as many cages as the number of tarantulas that you want to keep. Two tarantulas should not be kept in one cage; otherwise the stronger one will kill the weaker one.

If you think that the lid of your spider's cage does not tightly cover it, giving the tarantula the opportunity to escape captivity, I will advise you to place a weighty object like a rock on top of the cage to forestall any possibility of the animal escaping. Note that tarantula birdeaters are very large and weighty. Its weight can pull out a loose lid.

Remove any vertical objects from your cage. The hide and substrate are enough. This will save him from the temptation of climbing up. They are not as skilful as arboreal tarantulas when it comes to climbing trees and vertical objects.

Always provide a tarantula birdeater with live prey or a diet that is suitable to their age, size and kind. For example, goliath birdeaters can kill mice for food but it is not advisable to give live mice or even big insects to young giant birdeaters. All animals also have the instinct of self-preservation. Every prey will always struggle and resist being killed by the predator until it is subdued. This struggle can sometimes result in serious injury to the predator. So, you can avoid exposing your tarantula to risk of injury by providing it with prey they can easily kill.

Take time to learn the moulting signs so that you will be able to differentiate them from death curl and symptoms of sickness.

Don't provide chlorinated water to your tarantula. Ordinary water is ok. Don't waste your money on bottled water unless you can afford it. Similarly, you should also avoid serving them with prey caught in a farm or around a garden treated with insecticides.

Tarantulas in general are not companion pets. No matter how gentle a tarantula is, you cannot play with it. The best you can do is to spend time watching the animal feed and spend its time in its cage. So, don't play with it and don't allow your children or visitors to do so. On no account should you handle your tarantula when it is moulting. In fact, the best practice is to allow the spider some peaceful moments during moulting. It is not the time to show the animal to your visitors.

Tarantulas, like all other arachnids, do not like light. They are nocturnal animals and hunters. So, you don't have to add auxiliary lighting in your tarantula cage. Note that your spider can become skittish and stressed if its cage is well illumined. Check the section on the light requirements and stick to the advice provided there.

The goliath birdeater is a species of tarantula but it has its unique behaviour. What may not constitute any danger to another species of tarantula may constitute a threat to a giant birdeater. So, when you seek for advise and search for information, especially on feeding and care, make sure that the tips you obtain are for a giant birdeater and not for any other species of tarantula. For example, it is a sound practice to include bamboo sticks, vertical objects and flowers in the cage of an arboreal tarantula. But such a practice is not recommended in the cage of a tarantula birdeater or any other terrestrial spider or burrowing tarantulas.

Tarantulas are not messy but this does not mean that you should not be cleaning their cage when they become dirty, or at least once in four months.

Things You Will Need

If you are starting in tarantula husbandry, there are important tools and equipment that you will require to have a rewarding experience. Below is the list of items that you have to get ready before you can order a pet goliath birdeater.

- The cage, which may be an aquarium or any suitable container obtained from the home
- A bowl for water
- A suitable substrate material
- The hideout such as a slab
- Food such as a live cricket
- Thermometer for measuring the temperature and hygrometer for measuring the humidity
- Heating equipment such as a reptile heat pad

You can see from the above that not much equipment is required to keep a tarantula. Starting in tarantula husbandry is not an expensive project.

How Much Does It Cost to Keep a Goliath Birdeater?

The purchase cost of a Goliath spider primarily depends on which species you are getting. As a general average, however, a good starter or beginner goliath spider can cost anywhere from $10/£8 to upwards of $500/£383 for an adult of a more rare species. Start-up costs could average around $95/£81, broken down as follows:

- Purchase price $20/£16
- 10 gallon aquarium $20/£16
- Light fixture $20/£16
- Bulb $10/£8
- Automatic timer $10/£8
- Cage accessories (substrate, starter burrows, water dish, etc.) $15/£11
- Total $90/£81

Of course, this is quite different from the yearly maintenance, on which you can probably expect to spend around $90/£69 each year. These would involve costs for the following:

- Food $50/£43

- Lamp bulbs $20/£16

- Cage accessories $20/£16

- Total $90/£76

Note that these are just general estimates and you may find yourself spending more or less depending on your unique circumstances and the available resources in your area. One other potential cost you should consider investing in are good books on the care of goliath spiders. Books are likely to be your most expensive purchases, but for the truly dedicated hobbyist or keeper, they can also be your most important investment.

Warnings!

Many people don't like spiders and they become startled when they see one. Therefore, on no account should you use your tarantula to frighten any person including your child and visitor. Don't allow anyone, especially someone that is afraid of a tarantula, to handle it. This is because such a person can throw the tarantula on the ground out of fear and this may result in injury to your spider.

Don't handle your tarantula. But if it is necessary that you handle it, you have to put on your gloves and make sure that you wash your hands with soap. Don't touch your eyes until your hands are properly washed as advised above. This is to avoid the possibility of the urticating hairs entering your eyes.

Know when your tarantula is charged and ready to bite. This will help you to avoid being bitten by your pet.

Don't allow your children to handle or feed your goliath birdeater. They are not a good species suitable for children handling.

Avoid over-feeding your tarantula birdeater. When a goliath birdeater eats more than what it should, the abdomen will bulge out. Given the nature of the abdomen of a spider, it can rupture easily from falls or by sharp objects.

Make sure that your tarantula's cage has opening for better air circulation. But the opening should be tiny as advised above.

Needless to say, a potentially venomous and dangerous creature such as this should never be allowed too much contact with other pets – especially mammals that can prove too eager and that might pose a threat to it. The spider might react aggressively or defensively. While the venom of Goliath spiders is not always fatal to humans, the same cannot be said of its effect on smaller mammals.

Besides, smaller mammals and reptiles are good meals for tarantulas. Therefore, they should in no case be allowed contact with your goliath birdeater. The potential danger is also true in reverse; that is larger pets such as dogs, cats or even mice and reptiles, can also cause harm to your pet spider, injuring them or even eating them outright. The bottom line is that goliath spiders should never be allowed outside of their enclosure unsupervised and should in no case be allowed to mingle with other pets.

Chapter 9: Ecology of Tarantulas

Goliath birdeaters are among the largest species of tarantula. They can kill large insects, some lizards and rodents with their venoms. But they are not the last man standing in the struggle for survival that characterise life in the jungle. In the ecosystem service, giant tarantulas eat different kinds of small animals such as invertebrates like crickets and cockroaches, reptiles like small lizards and snakes. But they also have their natural enemies. There are a lot of animals that prey on them. In this chapter, I am going to tell you more about the natural predators and prey of tarantulas.

Goliath Birdeater Prey

I talked about goliath birdeater food in details. So, there isn't much to add here. I only need to mention that goliath birdeaters are not vegetarians. They feed on other animals including spiders. They are cannibals as well. So, in the ecosystem, small mammals, reptiles and invertebrates constitute their major foods. They are called goliath birdeaters but in reality, they rarely eat birds. They are given the name birdeater based on an 18th century engraving of a Spanish explorer in which a member of the family of giant birdeater is shown consuming birds. Though, they can eat small birds and chickens, but these do not constitute their major foods.

Natural Enemies of Goliath Tarantulas

Just as giant birdeaters prey on many animals, so do many other animals prey on them to maintain equilibrium in nature. Here are the various predators of goliath birdeaters.

Mammals

Many mammals, including man, kill spiders of various kinds including some tribal people. However, Theraphosa blondi essentially constitutes a good meal for a number of mammals such as weasels, coyotes, shunks, and even humans. Some of these mammals look for the burrows of these spiders and dig them out in order to kill and feed on them. Some traditional folks of north-eastern South America and some other tribal people in some other parts of the world use tarantulas to prepare certain delicacies. First, they singe the urticating bristles and then wrap it in banana leaves before roasting it. It has a flavour that is similar to that of shrimp.

Reptile predators

Though goliath birdeaters can kill and eat small lizards, they are also consumed by large lizards and snakes. However, the choice of goliath birdeaters as food can turn out to be harmful to a reptile because some tarantula birdeaters can actually kill reptiles of a considerable size.

Birds

As already mentioned above, birds are not actually the major food of these spiders even though the term birdeater is attached to their name. Certain birds such as eagles, hawks and owls feed on these spiders once they find them.

Insects

The inclusion of insects among the predators of giant tarantulas may be actually surprising to some people. This is because it constitutes the major meals of tarantula. The truth is that only a few insects can kill a tarantula. The major insect predator of tarantulas is the spider wasp, also known as the pepsis or tarantula hawk. This flying insect normally stings a tarantula to paralyse it with its poison. It will then bring it inside its nest. It uses the abdomen of a tarantula as its brooding space. The insect opens the abdomen of its victim, lays just one egg there and seal it the nest. It can also use the spider's burrow as its nest, which it will cover after laying its egg. The egg will hatch into larva and begins to feed on the abdomen of the tarantula. But surprisingly, it does not eat up the vital organs of its prey so that it will not die. It will keep feeding on it until it becomes an adult, when it will come out from the abdomen.

Flies and other parasites

Certain types of flies, just like tarantula hawks, lay their eggs on the body of the tarantula. When the eggs are hatched and metamorphose into pupae, they begin to feed on the abdomen of the tarantula after bursting it open. With a ruptured abdomen, the GB will definitely die. When I was discussing the diseases and medical conditions of a tarantula birdeater, I included parasites like mites in the list. They can live on their bodies and feed on them though they may not kill their host like these flies and pepsis.

Invertebrates

Invertebrates like giant centipedes can kill and feed on tarantulas. With their claws, they are able to paralyse tarantulas and species of spiders. They can crawl through holes. A certain species of cricket called bulldog raspy cricket is strong enough to engage a tarantula in a fight and comes out victorious. It has strong and razor-like mandibles. The spines on its limbs are as sharp as a knife.

So, if you are keeping a goliath tarantula or any other species of tarantula, ensure that you keep your tarantula cage in a location where these natural predators cannot get at. You should also cover the cage of your tarantula with a lid and place a heavy object on it. The holes by the sides and on the tops of the cage should also be very tiny so that these natural predators will not have any access to their cage.

Resources

As a beginner, I strongly suggest that you join a tarantula enthusiast society or an online forum. Here are links to some online forums to join.

Note: at the time of printing, all the websites below were working. As the Internet changes rapidly, some sites might no longer be live when you read this book. That is, of course, out of our control.

Online forum

www.tarantulaforum.com

https://tomsbigspiders.com

http://arachnoboards.com/

http://atshq.org/forum/index.php

https://groups.yahoo.com/neo/groups/arachnid_world/info

http://www.arachnoboards.com/ab/

http://tealizard.com/forum/index.php

Enthusiast Group and Society

The American Tarantula Society (ATS) – http://www.atshq.org

British Tarantula Society (BTS) – http://wwwthebts.co.uk

Made in the USA
Las Vegas, NV
19 November 2020